"Surviving Chaos: Wow, ____ __ timely concept!

As we are entering the greatest chaos of the past 75 years, the time has come for application of the primary support for life itself, Divine Love."

C. Norman Shealy, M.D., Ph.D.
Professor of Energy Medicine
President Emeritus,
Holos University Graduate Seminary

Founding President,
American Holistic Medical Association

"Bob has captured the essence of "What Life Is All About" and how we are all connected with a spiritual bond to each other with Divine Love. We all have part of this wonderful power of Divine Love, but don't know how to use it to solve our problems. Bob gives detailed, word by word examples,of how to use the power of Divine love for ourselves, and in working in groups, to achieve what most will call miracles.

A must read for all in these times of increasing personal and worldwide Chaos."

John V Milewski Ph.D.
Author, The Crystal Source Book
Awarded 30 patents
Smithsonian Recipient

"Robert Fritchie brings us a series of approaches for healing ourselves, our global community and our planet. Surviving Chaos is a timely book, considering the unprecedented local and global threats that humans are posing to ourselves. These, on top of our often limited capacities to deal with stress, leave us vulnerable to distress and to the disruptions in our lives that stresses can produce. This book will show you how tapping into our intuitive and spiritual awarenesses can bring about dramatic healings on all levels of our existence. As with any powerful new approach, you will want to take this step by careful step, particularly in learning to rely on muscle testing."

Daniel J. Benor, M.D.
Author of Healing Research, Volumes 1-3 and
Seven Minutes to Natural Pain Release

"This is one of the most important and effective teachings for helping suffering humanity in the imminent crises ahead. Bob Fritchie and I have worked together before with Divine Love group healing processes, but his latest techniques - as taught in this book- allow *any* spiritually open individual or group to petition the Creator to assist us in changing what man has polluted, destroyed or exploited. "This is the ultimate 21st Century healing manual!"

Bruce Eric Hedendal, D.C., FICS, DAAPM, Ph.D.

"Chief Engineer Robert Fritchie has given to the world a sparkling, vibrant, virtual creative engine, that works with and through Mankind's bioplasmatic scaffolding allowing incarnations of our highest intentions and true abilities!

You are reading 30+ years of distilled experience. I was there for some of this.

The Uber Spiritual Scientist, Marcel Vogel, might say his best student has created a masterpiece. A masterpiece by an Engineer.

Let us retrieve our organic heritage on this Planet. Let Mankind not fail the final examination for continuance of existence in Universe. Go ahead, loosen your genius, Save the Planet, Save our Garbage Dumps, Pull our heads out our Collective Behinds and wake up!!!! The first signs of Degeneration are appearing in Mother Earth, Creatress of Life. Become aligned with the Unseen Creative Force of Universe. Turn off your TV. Create Your Future. Literally, we have to Create Our Future.

This tome will give you the Life Code of Manifestation, in a simple arithmetic sentence. A+"

John J. Adams, M.D.
Bioplasmatic Cynbernetics
Sedona, Arizona

"Proven Self-Healing Techniques from a Facilitator whose motive is Compassion and Love-Wisdom. Written in a direct format, which is easy to read, understand, and apply - all signs of a facilitator who has proven these modalities to be safe and successful in the Laboratory of Life. Thanks for revealing these techniques to the world."

Mario De La Garza, Teacher and Writer,
The Synthetic-Wisdom

"Bob approaches the realm of healing with the compassionate soul and intuition of a shaman while maintaining the objective clarity of a scientist. He brings science and spirituality together in a way that any reader can appreciate and understand."

John Sase, Ph.D., Economics

SURVIVING CHAOS:

HEALING WITH

DIVINE LOVE

A Spiritual
Energy Healing Process

Robert G. Fritchie

World Service Institute
Knoxville, Tennessee

Library of Congress Control Number: 2009922025

ISBN 978-0-9819513-7-9

Fritchie, Robert
Surviving Chaos: Healing With Divine Love
A Spiritual Energy Healing Process
1st edition March 2009
editor: Katy Koontz

1. Mind and body. 2. Spirituality. 3. Spiritual healing. 4. Energy healing. 5. Self-help techniques.

CONTENTS

CONTENTS

Surviving Chaos: Healing With Divine Love

CONTENTS

Surviving Chaos: Healing With Divine Love

CONTENTS

"Life is really simple, but
we insist on making it
complicated."

Confucius

INTRODUCTION

Our world is spiraling rapidly out of control. Despite major achievements in medicine, science, and global business, whole nations and their infrastructure are eroding as we continue to forfeit our ethics and integrity. There is startling evidence that our very existence is being threatened by an increase in potential disasters: solar radiation, droughts, terrorism, and nuclear threats. Food and water are already polluted or are becoming so, and shortages are on the increase. Human rights violations are abysmal. We have witnessed a general deterioration in society through the shocking outbreaks of random killings by young people in schools and on colleges campuses. The pressure and stress in our society and elsewhere is creating mental imbalance in the family unit.

Humanity is at an important crossroads. We have come a long way in a very short time in our recorded history. Yet today we face great challenges in environmental pollution, health, finance, security, education, and well-being that have been ignored for so long that the solutions are now controversial, life-threatening and very costly.

Surviving Chaos: Healing With Divine Love

It is evident that we have not solved many of the key problems plaguing the world's population. And it does not appear that we will make a difference following only mental solutions. However, we submit that there are spiritual solutions, and *you* are needed to help implement the changes needed.

Affecting Change

A lecturer on behavioral psychology once said:

People do *not* change until the pain of *not* changing *exceeds* the pain of changing.

How bad is your pain? Are you interested in learning how to *change* things with minimum pain? Do you have the desire to help yourself and humanity? Or do you think that you can continue to ignore your pain, your family's pain, and the pain of your neighbors, countrymen, and other nations as the world careens toward all kinds of catastrophes from which we may not be able to recover?

Why This Book?

This book offers solutions that you can implement right now to help yourself and others to make the changes necessary to preserve or attain collective well-being.

INTRODUCTION

This is not a typical self-help book. It is a concise explanation of how to use the combined energy of a group of ordinary citizens to make improvements in life-threatening situations, environment pollution, and dangerous mass behavior. Some of the topics will shock you. You may sit dumbfounded and wonder why no one has ever told you about your birthright as a human being.

Set aside your disbelief and study these chapters. It only takes a small group to effect the *change* needed.

Beginning in 1980, we (my colleagues and I) started a long-term scientific study using natural energy to heal the human body. That study produced phenomenal natural healing techniques that worked, but to put them into practice required that the public be educated about human energy. We did this successfully and trained more than a thousand health care practitioners from various disciplines. I developed a healing program, the Divine Love Group Healing Process (DLGHP), and improved it over more than twenty-odd years until I had perfected a teaching format that the public could use effectively.

I taught the "Process," as I call it, both privately and in workshops until 2008, when I decided to publish it as a training program on the Internet. The response has been amazing! We found that people are eager to learn how to help themselves.

My original plan was to take our teaching to the next

level in an advanced program that would show people how to apply the Process to solve life-threatening health and environmental problems that threaten all our lives. I decided to accelerate that timetable and make the advanced teachings available worldwide so that people could begin to benefit immediately.

Chapter 1 identifies a number of highly probable events that may upset your life. You will be shown many things that you can do to help yourself and your family to survive in these difficult times.

Have you ever been given so much conflicted information that you could not separate fact from fiction? In **Chapter 1** you will also be introduced to a simple Self-Truth Test technique that you can use to evaluate the truth about your health.

In **Chapter 2** you will be exposed to a set of New Realities that may shock you. We are going to cover material in this book that in the unseen world is called "energy." Please set aside any impulse to dismiss this new information and keep an open mind. The techniques described in the following chapters are meant to help you. However, you must apply the techniques to get results.

The following is a simple Personal Energy Equation that describes what you need to make change happen.

$$S + DL + P + F = \textit{Change}$$

INTRODUCTION

You do not have to be good at math to use the Equation. It is simply a memory aid to help you get results. We will explain the Equation's meaning and how to use it in **Chapters 3 -7**. In these chapters you will learn how to apply amazing natural energy principles to facilitate *change*. Some of the advanced material we cover may apply directly to you. You will be able to observe the results as beneficial *change* in your own life. Other topics that you can influence and help *change* require the participation of a group of well-meaning people.

In **Chapter 8**, you will learn how you can apply the Equation to *change* specific applications in life and the environment.

In **Chapter 9**, we will explore ways to make *change* more effective.

Chapter 10 and 11 are for your review and study of the **DLGHP Training Course** that thousands of people are currently using.

"Never doubt that a small group of thoughtful, committed citizens can change the world. Indeed, It is the only thing that ever has."

Margaret Mead

Chapter 1 - BE AWARE

Current Events

Major events are happening that need your attention and participation. Our civilization is in decline because of negligent acts by the world populace that continue to cause energetic imbalances in the world.

The world is experiencing severe droughts that are producing shortages in potable water and food-crop production. The severity of storms, earthquake activity, and melting glaciers are all harbingers of unwanted change. We cannot stop these effects, but we can learn to maintain ourselves with less hardship.

As earth changes continue to manifest world-wide, governments may be unable to respond effectively enough to relieve human suffering, as evidenced by recent responses to earthquakes, hurricanes, cyclones, and tsunamis. Therefore, we must learn how to care for ourselves if we are denied support services.

You can watch these events unfold around you and feel victimized by the potential physical hardships and mental turmoil, or you can learn how to take care of yourself and your family.

This book gives you the tools to survive in the difficult times ahead. It is your opportunity to understand and apply perfectly natural principles in energy to change your life and help yourself. The choice is yours.

By now you may be thinking, "What could possibly happen beyond the worldwide financial market deterioration that could affect me?" Let's look at some facts together.

Unwanted Changes

Sun Flare Radiation is occurring, emitting harmful radiation. This radiation has high-energy effects on the human body and acts like nuclear radiation to mutate or kill body cells. This is not simply a bad sunburn; it can be lethal. Scientists are cautious about discussing this in public because there is no inexpensive physical solution.

Solar radiation bursts are so strong that they can disrupt and destroy communication satellites. Think about this. Ground Positioning Systems (G.P.S.) can go "blind" meaning that we can lose the ability to track anything that uses G.P.S.—ships at sea, airplanes, cars, etc. You may think this does not affect you directly, but it does. If goods and lives are lost, transportation and the economy stagnate.

The solar radiation hazard to people may increase. Did you know that during past solar bursts, astronauts on the space station sought protection in a specially shielded part of the ship? What do you think may happen to you if you happen to be flying at 35,000 feet and are exposed to this radiation? No one dares hazard a guess, but many commercial pilots are wearing radiation detectors. These particles go through almost everything, so staying indoors is not a viable solution unless your house is sheathed in lead plate.

Terrorism continues to spread world-wide and terrorists want to kill all who do not believe in their ideology. Do you want to help stop hatred? Do you want to learn how you can continue to function if your water or public services are interrupted?

Nuclear Bomb Threats are real. Every country wants a bomb, but not every country should have one. The problem is what happens to us and to our environment if a nuclear bomb goes off where we live. We do not have to incur an attack directly on a populated area to totally disrupt a population. Simply allowing a bomb to be detonated at a high altitude could cause radioactive particles to be carried across many countries by the jet streams. The fallout could poison people, animals, crops, and water everywhere in the radioactive fallout path.

Surviving Chaos: Healing With Divine Love

Electromagnetic Pulses are real. If a nuclear bomb were large enough, it would put forth an electromagnetic pulse that could destroy every computer chip within range. This isn't just a problem for your personal computer. Computer chips control automobile circuits, power plant and chemical plant electronics, and control systems of every imaginable type. Even your household gadgets have these chips.

Consider this. One morning you wake up and you have no power to operate your home or car. There would be no way to drive to a supermarket to buy food. Even if you walked, not much would be left for you to buy, because supply trucks would not be able to restock inventories. The affected areas would come to a sudden standstill. *What would you do?* The prospects are not pleasant, to be sure. The pulse may not harm us directly, but it would certainly have a devastating effect upon the quality of life.

Food Shortages prevail throughout the world. Drought, poor soil, and plant infestations are destroying crops and diminishing the nutritional value of those that remain.

This book offers you a natural energy healing system that you can apply to yourself, your family, and others. We will show you how to achieve *changes* that may help save your life and the lives of your loved ones.

Are You Willing To Learn?

When people first hear about something that is new to them, the common tendency is to reject the information. People say, "Why haven't I heard about this before? Who is using this? Does it work? Is it safe? What do I do first?"

We could write an entire book on the various healing modalities that exist around the world, but that is not our intent here. Rather, I would like you to educate yourself. Apply the principles we give you in this book so that you can improve your life and survive. To improve your confidence in this information, you need to know three things:

1. The author of this book is a professional chemical engineer with thirty years of research experience in human energy studies and energy healing. The information provided has been widely applied by people in our workshops.

2. Many people regularly employ the energy healing methods given in this book with excellent results.

3. You need to have a way of self-testing for the truth in what you hear or read that is tamper-proof. You cannot depend upon the opinions of others in this work because every person injects both bias and personal beliefs into everything they say or do. The truth is within you. All you need to do is to be able to access it.

Surviving Chaos: Healing With Divine Love

Self-Truth Test

Muscle testing is an interactive method that you can use by yourself to get to the truth that affects you. John Diamond, M.D., was the first to widely test these techniques. Diamond became quite famous as a pioneer in muscle testing with his book, *Your Body Doesn't Lie*. When used correctly, muscle testing will point you to the truth.

David R. Hawkins, M.D., Ph.D., author of *Power vs. Force*, conducted double-blind studies wherein neither the tester nor the person being tested knew about, or could see, the materials being tested. The experiments showed that the human body gives accurate responses to test questions regarding all sorts of topics. This knowledge is already stored in the body's cells. Muscle testing merely allows you to access it. When the testing is done correctly, people can get accurate answers to health related questions.

Bruce Lipton, Ph.D., a tenured professor at the University of Wisconsin's School of Medicine, has confirmed through lab experiments that human cells carry information. He details this in his book, *The Biology of Belief*, which is well worth reading.

We suggest you use muscle-testing techniques to test for the spiritual and physical truth of anything dealing with your personal health that concerns you. This is a test method that you do for yourself, all by yourself. While it is accurate for testing topics that are for your highest good, it cannot be used successfully for prophecy, manipulation of people or events, or to gain financial advantage. For example, you cannot use this test to try to get guidance on winning numbers in the lottery, what stocks to invest in, or which relationships you should pursue. You can, however, use muscle testing to determine that a food or beverage (or anything that you consume or breathe) is safe for you to ingest.

How To Do Your Self-Truth Test (muscle test)

Here is how you self-test. Form a ring with the first finger and thumb of your strongest (or dominant) hand, as in Figure 1.

Figure 1   **Figure 2**

Hook the first finger of your other hand over the ring at the point where the first finger and thumb of the ring come together, as in Figure 2.

The idea is to ask yourself a test question that you can answer with a simple *yes* or *no*. If the answer is *yes*, then it is hard to pull the ring open with the single finger. If the answer is *no*, it is easy to pull the ring open.

Calibrate your strength response using refined sugar. We all know that an excess of sugar is not good for us. Prove this to yourself by asking yourself, "Is an excess of refined sugar good for my body?" You will get a *no* answer as evidenced by the ring opening easily as you pull on it. This is not a strength test. Do not force the ring open, but do use steady pressure.

Try something else that you know is good for you, perhaps an apple, to get a feeling for a *yes* answer. The ring will *not* easily open and should stay closed. If you are forcing or pulling it open, use less finger strength to hold the ring closed.

Once you practice several times, you can start to ask your body questions about the spiritual and physical truthfulness of whatever you are reading or hearing from others that applies to your health.

Some questions are inappropriate because they are outside the realm of your human cellular knowledge. If you are unsure of the appropriateness of a question you want answered, ask instead if your proposed question will yield a truthful response. If the answer is *yes*, then continue by asking the question.

For example, you want to know if your sick sister is about to die. You want to ask the question, "Is Sue going to die soon?" You realize that there is no basis for your cells to know what is going on in someone else's body. Ask instead, "If I ask about Sue's life expectancy, will I get a spiritually and physically accurate answer?" Generally the answer will be a *no*.

You can use muscle testing to validate the spiritual and physical truth contained in every sentence of this book. You can also evaluate whether or not a particular paragraph, sentence, or word applies to you directly.

Please pay close attention to muscle testing, because it will enable you to self-test the truth and goodness of things for the rest of your life. If you use the healing system presented later in this book to correct something you eat or drink, you will definitely want to confirm that the correction is complete before you consume anything.

Definitions

Before we go further, we want to define some common terms used in the book. They are shown in bold headings below. These are our definitions. They are purposely simplified so we can concentrate on the real message without controversy.

Mind is an unseen energy field interspersed in and around the human body. Mind works like a hologram to store memories of life experiences. These experiences operate like a reference library or tape recorder that affects future individual behavior.

For example, if a young child is bitten by a barking dog, the fear-based memory of the bite is stored in the child's Mind. It is common for that child to be afraid of dogs even as an adult. The irony is that the adult may not recall why he or she is afraid but may flinch or recoil at the sound of a dog barking.

Mind responds to thought, but Mind can also misinterpret. Mind does not know spiritual and physical truth until that truth is revealed. A person can receive untrue input and go through life making decisions based upon that false information. If you muscle test for truth, and the truth is different now from the truth that you based decisions upon, then you need to replace a stored experience with spiritual truth. That replacement only occurs in Mind when directed to do so by the Soul. You will read more about this and more about how to do it later in this book.

Mental Energy is a term some people use to explain energy healing. An individual can use his or her Mind to conduct healings, but doing so has two potential downsides.

First, the body has a real energetic charge, just like a battery. The battery-like energy of the healer's body can decrease if his mental energy is used to do healing work on other people or things.

Second, a person giving or receiving healing help can limit healing results because Mind injects its limited beliefs into the healing. Therefore, the recipient of the healing may not receive the correct energy level or quantity of healing energy. Thus, end results are less effective using Mind rather than Soul energy.

Religion is the establishment of belief systems and practices based upon various religious teachers and documents. Most religions are derived from Master Teachers such as Buddha, Christ, Krishna, and Mohammad, as well as other revered persons. A religious person may or may not be spiritual. You do not have to be a member of a particular faith to participate in healing work. People of all faiths have the same opportunity.

Spirituality is not a religion. Spirituality is the acknowledgment of a Divine energy and Divine intelligence in the universe that has been called many things over many centuries. Most spiritual people try to behave in a manner that honors that Divine energy. Hence, a person can be spiritual without being religious. By observation, you may have already determined that some members of religions are not very spiritual.

Soul is an energy from the Creator that is interspersed in and around a human being that stores *spiritual teachings* gathered during one's lifetime rather than a record of *all life experiences* stored by Mind. Some people believe that the Soul moves through various lifetimes. Others believe that the Soul disintegrates when physical life ends. Some people do not believe the Soul even exists because they cannot see or sense it. Some people believe this definition applies to Spirit.

Spirit Is the energy connection between the Soul and the Infinite Intelligence that we call the Creator. Incidentally, what's commonly called "spiritual truth" is true for everyone, regardless of age, sex, nationality, or individual beliefs. Thus, we are all connected together via Spirit to the Creator. Some believe this definition is for the Soul.

Spiritual Energy is defined as energy from the Creator of the universe that a person can process through his or her own Soul. A person who believes in a Soul and uses his or her conscious intention to employ the Soul in facilitating healing finds these efforts are effective. The benefits of using Soul-based spiritual energy are the following:

1. Soul energy is not diminished by the presence of limited beliefs stored in the Mind.

2. Any healing facilitated as a Soul does not deplete personal body energy. The body continuously recharges through Soul.

3. Your Soul can transmit tremendous energetic power to facilitate *change*. Soul energy far exceeds Mind energy.

Chapter 2 - NEW ENERGY REALITIES

What I am going to explain here has been known by certain world teachers for thousands of years. To keep you from claiming your own spiritual energetic power, the truth about how the universe works has been kept from you. So before you dive in to start making *changes*, let's look at five energy realities that you may not know about.

1. Current reality is what you can make happen in the present; that reality changes with your experience.

My spiritual journey started forty years ago with the Japanese martial art of Aikido (meaning "the spiritual way"). In about 1967, Morihei Uyeshiba, the founder of Aikido, sent Kanai Sensei and Yamada Sensei, two young Japanese Aikido Masters, to the United States. Kanai Sensei started teaching in Cambridge, MA, with about a dozen students. I made a career move to Cleveland and also studied under Yamada Sensei, whose dojo (school) had about 25 members.

We eventually learned how to use "Ki" (spiritual

energy) in our bodies to move an opponent, using only minimal contact. We learned how to to enter a fully conscious state where we could endure heat, cold, and pains such as those resulting from direct punches and nerve holds. We also learned to apply Ki to promote rapid recovery from injuries, including knee dislocations.

While it was obvious that Aikido tapped an unseen energy that could be called upon to produce physical and psychological effects, the *how* and *what* of that energy was not explained. Students of Ki, Chi, Prana, shaman energy, Native American Medicine, and Reiki access the same universal energy source at various levels depending upon their training and personal energy purification. The concept of *love* energy is not evident in most of these therapeutic approaches.

Energy Reality #1 is the essence of human growth and development. It took me many years to understand and apply this martial art principle to everything in my life.

2. The energy of the universe is everywhere; we can all tap into that energy and use it appropriately.

So what exactly does this mean? To grasp the significance, consider these facts:

Acupuncture is an energy healing method developed

by the Chinese thousands of years ago. It is based upon treating energy meridians (pathways) found in the human body. Today that process has spread to the West and is routinely administered. It works!

Tai Chi is another Chinese system of exercises to circulate the energy of the universe through the body. The concept is that the life force energy keeps one in good energetic balance. People of all ages in China practice this art on a daily basis to maintain tranquility and health. It works!

QiGong is an amazing Chinese martial art. One can see a Master using energy to move objects toward or away from him. In China, QiGong is used in many hospitals to deaden physical pain so that surgical patients do not require anesthesia. This is cost effective and allows a patient to recover without side effects. It works!

3. Proof that energy follows thought:

Marcel Vogel was a well known IBM senior materials scientist. He held patents on liquid crystal technology and developed the coating that made large capacity computer hard drives a reality. Marcel shifted his interest in later years to the study of human energy. Some of his ground-breaking experiments are described below.

I was privileged to help Marcel. We lectured

throughout the United States separately and together for many years sharing the results of our healing research.

Natural quartz crystals exhibit a piezoelectric physical property. This means that if you squeeze a crystal it will give off an electrical charge that can be used. For example, crystal transducers are used in reservoir dam construction to measure compressive force. They are used in gas grills to produce a spark to light the grill. Crystals operate at a variety of frequencies; in the early days of radio, "crystal radios" were the rage. Today, we produce synthetic crystals and make them into computer chips.

Marcel Vogel had a lab in San Jose at IBM that was full of highly sensitive equipment. One day he decided to see if he could transmit human energy across space to a measuring instrument. He held a common quartz crystal in his hand and breathed deeply. As he did this, the crystal came into resonant balance with Marcel's body energy. Then Marcel pointed the crystal at a photomultiplier tube located across his lab. The tube was hooked up to a display capable of detecting a charge transfer.

When Marcel pulsed his breath, the crystal transmitted a charge to the tube that could be seen as a point of light. *Marcel's experiment showed that energy could be moved through space with intention.*

From his laboratory in Japan, **Masaru Emoto** has

helped people to understand the effect of intention on a very profound basis using water crystals. His work demonstrates three realities:

A. "Love" is an energy that can be transferred into water. Frozen water crystals containing negative thoughts or harmful chemicals display ugly patterns in the ice crystal samples that Emoto photographs. Yet, when people use their intention to direct thoughts of "love" to contaminated water, the water is changed, resulting in beautiful crystal patterns that look like snowflakes.

B. Emoto drew the word LOVE on a piece of paper that was then attached to a bottle of contaminated water. The energy of love from the symbol alone was transferred into the water sample. The resulting photographs of the water crystals were beautiful. The water had been changed.

C. Water crystals containing the energy of love displayed a unique hexagon form with very ornamental clusters at each point of the hexagon. Emoto proved that his results are repeatable. When people in other labs repeated the experiments using their own water sources, the results yielded the same characteristics; the water had been changed by the intention of love.

4. Directed thought energy is not limited by distance, and effects can be instantaneous.

A. Some Indian holy men have taught that healing can be obtained through the use of symbols printed on paper that a person in need holds in their hand. The intention of the holy man for correcting that person's problem is transferred from the holy man to the recipient who may be miles away. It works!

B. In another experiment, Marcel Vogel showed that an X-ray film of a person could be used to repair damage to that person, even if the person was many miles away. I saw this done in 1980 in San Jose, CA, when a person with broken bones was healed remotely.

C. Clive Baxter did an intention experiment with plants and projected thought. He showed that a plant would respond electrically to human thought by emitting a signal that could be measured. The signal showed smooth, positive sine-like waves in the presence of happy thoughts. The plant responded with a ragged saw-tooth, low-amplitude wave in the presence of a harmful thought directed to the plant.

Vogel repeated Baxter's experiment using a philodendron plant hooked up to a lie detector. When Vogel projected thoughts of love and well-being to the plant, the waveforms on the lie detector were smooth, large-amplitude waves. When Marcel projected the thought of tearing a plant leaf, the response was the same ragged display that Baxter saw. The difference here is that Marcel had coordinated a timed test with a doctor friend. This experiment was conducted with Marcel in India and the test apparatus and philodendron in San Jose, CA. Marcel's thoughts were *instantaneously transferred* to the plant and outputted in real time on the display! No telephones or radio contacts took place. *This proved that thought could be transferred through space without a time delay.*

D. Blood behaves like liquid crystals. During a medical doctor training session in the early 1980s, we watched a simultaneous split-screen video made from two lab experiments that Marcel Vogel had prepared using his $500,000 Zeiss microscope with attached video system.

The video on the left showed a bland gray amorphous liquid crystal. When Marcel applied electricity to the liquid crystal, a thick dark outline of a block numeral appeared, followed by a light flash, then the area filled in, becoming a solid black numeral.

The video on the right simultaneously showed a sample drop of blood from a person who was diseased. I think it was a cancer. Viewed through the Zeiss microscope, the drop had a ragged outline and colored blotches. When Marcel focused his intention and pulsed love to the blood sample, the outline became a smooth, thick-lined oval. Then a flash of light occurred, and the sample changed composition, now appearing healthy.

Both experiments behaved the same way - with a bold outline, followed by a light flash and a transformation to a new form. *This experiment showed that blood, behaving like a liquid crystal, can be energetically changed with the energy of love.*

5. Use the Creator's love in all that you do to avoid transmitting limited love energy to recipients.

In my early days of healing work, I worked with pain patients in a chiropractic doctor's clinic. None had been helped by traditional treatment. I directed love energy to them. The recipient (the person receiving a healing) was asked to pulse their breath to release whatever was responsible for their pain and then to draw in more love energy to restore their body.

All the patients released their pain, but a curious thing happened. The men were fine, but the women experienced a new pain that moved down their legs. Believing that the effect was a surface electrostatic energy discharge, the doctor had the women remove pantyhose and put on cotton hospital gowns. This corrected the moving pain problem, but it did not explain why the pain suddenly appeared in the legs.

Marcel Vogel had begun a series of weekend training programs for thirteen medical doctors to discuss his energy experiments and show the relevance of his findings. We discussed the female leg-pain effect with the doctor group.

John J. Adams, MD, asked to tour with me for a week. When he observed the difficulty with women recipients, he suggested using the Creator's love, rather than my love, in the healing service. To my amazement, the traveling leg pain that women had previously reported did not materialize.

I immediately realized that my definition of love was subject to my limited beliefs, which in turn limited the energy applied.

Review

Our scientific concept of healing energy transmission and distance is flawed. The energy of intention does not follow the current concept of space-time limitations (what we all think of as generally accepted reality). We see in the examples in this chapter that the effect of an intention begins immediately and operates without being limited by distance—whether the change is to someone or something in the same room or to a person or object 5000 miles away!

"There are only two ways to live your life. One is as though nothing is a miracle. The other is as though everything is a miracle."

Albert Einstein

Chapter 3 - THE SOUL

(The **S** in your Personal Energy Equation)

Let us see if we can agree on two points:

1. It does not matter in this discussion if you are a religious person who goes to a temple, church, shrine, mosque, or mountaintop in support of your religion or religious practices. The principles taught in this book apply to every man, woman, and child.

2. That which is defined as "spiritual" is from a higher plane, energy level, or frequency that we cannot see, measure, or fully comprehend. That spiritual state is the Infinite Source of all that is. It is Divine and is the God-head of all.

Spiritual teachers from the past to present day refer to two terms interchangeably: *spirit* and *soul.* It does not matter in this discussion which term you prefer to use.

We refer to Soul as an unseen energy form that resides in man. It witnesses whatever we do, but it does not direct our actions *unless we ask it to do so.*

Surviving Chaos: Healing With Divine Love

There was a great scene in a movie a few years back in which an idiot savant was asked to punctuate the following clause: that which is is that which is not is not. A strange clause indeed! The clause doesn't make much sense until you look at it spiritually. Then one might see this: "That which is, is. That which is not, is not!" That makes perfect sense now, doesn't it? **We need to realize that there are great spiritual truths in the universe. They are true whether we know about and agree with them or not**.

Many cultures teach that we are simply bodies seeking a spiritual connection higher than ourselves—that is, seeking a Divine presence located in the heavens or some higher plane of existence. Another way of looking at ourselves is to see that:

We are spiritual beings with a physical body. Part of the Creator is already present in us as our Soul.

As spiritual beings derived from the Creator, we are all entitled to be called children of the Creator. Every religious or spiritual person can call the Creator his or her Spiritual Father, and each of them would be right.

Even better, we can operate as true children of the Creator by claiming our spiritual *power* here on earth. We do this by indicating to ourselves that we are *using our Soul rather than our Mind* in all that we do, providing that we act in accordance with the Creator's will. That way two things become spiritually and physically true:

1. We bypass our ego should our Mind attempt to interfere. We operate as spiritual beings, not as the Creator, but infused with a piece of the Creator, through our Spirit and Soul.

2. We honor the energy of the Creator by using that same universal energy (we call it Divine Love) to facilitate *change*. We will examine more about this in the section about loving intention in Chapter 4.

By operating with a Soul-directed life, we can work effortlessly to affect *change*. Therefore please accept that you have a **Soul** and use it in all you do.

When we want to communicate with the Creator, we can use our Soul to make a direct connection through Spirit. In this sense, Spirit is like a personal telephone connection to the Creator.

"I find it interesting that the meanest life,
the poorest existence,
is attributed to God's will,
but as human beings become more affluent,
as their living standard and style begin to ascend the material scale,
God descends the scale of responsibility at a commensurate speed."

Maya Angelou

Chapter 4 - DIVINE LOVE

(The **DL** in your Personal Energy Equation)

Some people who have not been exposed to a spiritual concept of love energy want to argue about the meaning of words. I use the term **Divine Love** to refer to the most benevolent form of non-contact, energetic spiritual love that we can define to ourselves or someone else.

From our workshops, students offered definitions and their ideas about Divine Love. Here are the most noteworthy:

Divine Love is available to you even in your darkest moments.

Divine Love does not hurt you.

Divine Love heals you.

Divine Love does not judge or punish you.

Divine Love is unconditional. You do not have to do anything in return.

Divine Love does all the work.

Divine Love is everywhere.

Divine Love is the glue that holds the universe together.

Divine Love is needed to make changes.

Surviving Chaos: Healing With Divine Love

A full appreciation of Divine Love is beyond human comprehension.

Some people prefer other definitions such as:

Divine Love = Infinite energy = supernatural intelligence = all that is = the highest form of positive energy = the highest spiritual love in the universe = God's Love = Creator's Love = your spiritual deity's love

Pick the definition that you feel brings you closest to the highest and best energy that you can imagine on a spiritual plane of existence. Whatever you select will be correct. No one can define in words all that can be said to fully express the beauty, serenity, and power of Divine Love.

The key thought is this: Avoid limiting your use of Divine Love energy. Everything you need to know in your life lies within you as spiritually coded information that you can extract and use at will, provided that your Soul and intention are aligned with the Creator's love.

As you use these definitions and key thoughts to help yourself and others, you will better understand these concepts.

Some people say they do not believe in God, but they usually say they believe in an intelligence out there in the universe that is greater than them. We are not trying to sell you on a concept of a religion or a definition or name for the Creator. Perhaps you prefer one of these names:

Creator = God = your deity = infinite energy = divine intelligence

Pick whatever has the greatest meaning to you. Again, the name is not as important as your willingness to accept that a Creator exists. If you do not believe this, then this book cannot help you.

How Our Bodies Function

Our bodies work like a big battery. When we breathe deeply, we charge ourselves up. Most people do not breathe deeply. They forget to do so or feel self-conscious about it. Thus, they continue shallow breathing. Worse, their energy can become depleted during the work day as their vital energy drains away.

In fact, when I first started to do energy healing in 1980, I used my body energy as the source to do healing work. This worked fine, but it led to a major problem. If students did too many successive healings, they experienced extreme fatigue as their own body batteries ran down.

If one or more people standing near you is energy depleted, guess what happens? Those people can pull energy from you. They go home feeling energized, and you are left feeling tired. Sadly, most of us react to these conditions by withdrawing, or we try to protect ourselves, because we sense that something unwanted is happening to us.

If you regularly find yourself in meetings, you are subject to the combined stress energy of the group. If that group is generating anger or animosity, then you can become not only depleted, but also highly stressed as that negative energy collects on your outer surface. Your body may even experience a slimy feeling during a negative meeting. Sometimes you might find your hands or feet sweating profusely. It is the same symptom--your battery is running down!

Fortunately, you can take a simple action to avert and correct all of these conditions if you learn to use your internal "Love Switch."

Your Love Switch

This switch exists at two levels that you can control: mental and spiritual.

When your Love Switch is *on*, your body recharges from the universe, *regardless of your breathing style*. When you are emotionally bothered by something, the tendency is to isolate or protect yourself from the situation. This means that you consciously or unconsciously withhold spiritual and mental love from others. Unfortunately, when you withhold your spiritual love, the Love Switch goes *off* and you do not recharge your batteries.

When you suddenly tire, feel that someone is pulling energy from you, or feel slimed or stressed, do not run away or avoid people. Instead do this:

> Take a deep breath and hold it.
> Tell yourself to turn on your Love Switch
> and accept Divine Love.
> Let your breath out slowly.
> Take a few more slow deep breaths.

Your fatigue and stress should go away.

Stress is caused by the energy of thought. It can be directed to you by others or it can be caused by your own thinking that then stays in the vicinity of your system. If you do not take corrective action, stress will further act upon you to produce illness.

The deeper teaching is that when you keep your Love Switch *on*, you automatically recharge yourself, as well as those around you who are energy depleted.

As you increase in your understanding and trust that Divine Love will not hurt you, you can achieve immediate *changes* in your energy level using a Soul-based spiritual approach.

Simply tell yourself to *use your Soul to take in Divine*

Surviving Chaos: Healing With Divine Love

Love. If you are sensitive, you may feel an energy rush as Divine Love recharges your battery instantly.

Additional Skills

Here are three energy exercises you can do right now with what you have learned.

1. Clearing Negative Energy. Suppose you are about to go into a room where a lot of emotional energy (such as a heated argument) has been expended. Use your intention to clear the room of negative energy before you enter. Here is how to do it:

> Draw in and hold your breath.
> Tell yourself silently to turn *on* your
> Love Switch.
> Hold an intention *to clear the room with Love*
> and pulse your breath lightly to release your
> intention.

That's all it takes. And *you* can do it right now!

2. Clear People. Suppose that you are in a meeting and someone loses his temper. Do the same thing as above setting the intention to *surround the angry person with Love.* Then watch the anger diminish.

3. Warm Yourself. Have you heard about how Tibetan monks can sit bare-chested for hours in the cold and snow? You can learn to do it as well - and no, you do not have to be shirtless.

What the monks do is regulate the energy flow in their bodies. When a body begins to suffer from the cold, capillaries contract. If you keep the blood flow circulating in your limbs, they will remain warm. If you are getting cold, try the following exercise.

Place the first two fingers of your left hand on the outside of your left knee joint and place the first two fingers of your right hand on the outside of your right knee joint. To do this you will need to bend your knees and crouch slightly or sit down.

Keep your lips and mouth closed. Do not make sounds—no giggling allowed!

Breathe in deeply through the nose, hold your breath for about five seconds, and them breathe out slowly and completely.

Wait about five seconds, then repeat this breathing pattern (in, hold breath, out, hold breath) two more times for a total of three times. By then you should be warm! If not, breathe in and out deeply a few more times. Then release your fingers and stand up. That should do it.

Notice in the first two exercises that we used the word *love* not **Divine Love**. In the third exercise, we did not even mention the term *love*. We did that purposely so that you can do your own experimentation. Insert the phrase **Divine Love** in all three exercises and personally experience the differences in the results you achieve. In the third exercise, try thinking to yourself: *I am warming up with Divine Love.*

Personal Experience

I had a life-changing experience that solidified my understanding of the difference between my *personal spiritual love* and *Divine Love.* I would like to share it with you.

Many years ago, I was doing consulting work on a government project. People held a great deal of animosity toward me because I had been brought in to recover schedule and straighten out project problems. I even brought in my own management team to help.

Every morning, I had a meeting with the contractor and/or military personnel to report progress. As the project proceeded, it became evident that many problems needed to be corrected. The stress was incredible because of the rework to correct deficiencies that my team had uncovered.

From Monday to Friday, I worked 12 hours a day on the site. Friday night, I would fly home feeling like I was coming down with the flu. I was tired, and my head and body ached. My wife and I would walk the beaches. By Sunday evening, I would be recovered. After three months of this, my body was feeling the effects. I used my *personal* love to clear rooms and angry people to little avail because my Love Switch kept shutting off. The animosity toward our team increased.

One Wednesday evening, I almost crawled to get to my hotel room. I collapsed on the bed and cried out: "Dear God I can't take this anymore." Immediately, I felt like someone had pulled a sheet off my body. The stress, frustration, and fatigue were all gone. I got the message and the teaching! From that point on, I used *Divine Love* rather than *personal love* in all that I did in my professional career and in my healing service. In effect, I learned the hard way to leave my Love Switch *on* all the time. I suggest that you do so as well.

Again, please, remember to use the Creator's Divine Love in all that you do to avoid transmitting limited love energy.

Personal Translation of Divine Love

I bet by now that as a careful reader, you are thinking: *Earlier the author said that the universal energy described in Chapter 2 did not embrace Divine Love*, and you would be right. After all, in my early Aikido training we were not taught love. Yet the Ki energy principles worked within us. This led me to the idea that the universal energy that mystics, scientists, and modern-day authors are struggling to define is an energy that exists in a neutral state. That is, it is neither positive or negative until we try to use it. Our intention makes the difference. For example:

An advanced martial artist will use the universal energy to help himself. He or she may not be using a positive or a negative intention but is simply tapping into the natural energy to achieve something.

A spiritual person may try to define the universal energy as a *positive* energy that incorporates the best definition that he or she can accept for the Creator's Love (Divine Love). I believe that when we accept that universal energy as Divine Love with an intention that honors and respects the Creator, the universal energy becomes activated and helps us. If this were not so, everyone could simply think, *fix my arm with the universal energy*, and it would happen.

Perhaps some advanced people can do lasting healing work without acknowledging the Creator, but this is not a widespread practice.

In the next chapter, we shall see how to apply Divine Love to initiate *change*.

"When the power of love overcomes the love of power, the world will know peace."

Jimi Hendrix

Chapter 5 - THE PETITION

(The **P** in your Personal Energy Equation)

Intention

Major research projects afoot all across the world are studying the energy effects of intention. These efforts assume that "intention" is a new energy discovery tied to how we think, but it is not new. Remember that Marcel Vogel scientifically demonstrated many proofs concerning the reality of intention and how it can be transferred through space in the early 1980s. I witnessed and participated in many of these experiments and reviewed the data personally.

Many of the world's population are still not aware that they can transmit energy. Nor do they realize that they can have a large-scale energy effect upon another human being or physical matter using their intention.

Sadly, people are also still stuck in mind-sets where they are not aware of their own spiritual nature. They tend to see themselves as human victims dependent upon others for survival. It has not occurred to these people that help on a spiritual basis can and does override all limitations.

Intention has evolved over the years to mean different things. Many centuries ago, specific people were trained in energy work. Many of their practices were concealed from the general population to avoid losing control over the populace. The intention of those select few was to remain socially above and separate from the people who they served. Our intention here is to provide energetic tools that can help you and your family.

Prerequisites for Using Proper Spiritual Intention

I believe that Divine Love, as a building block for *change*. It is the energy of unconditional caring for all of us, emanating from the Creator to everything in the universe.

We must approach the Creator and Divine Love in the right manner—with respect, little ego, and a willingness to serve the common good rather than just ourselves. Plus we must surrender our lives and the results of our efforts to the Creator. When we do these things, we are able to interact with Divine Love to effect *change* in ways that you have only dreamed of before today. Thus, you have the option and an opportunity to directly participate. Your participation can help yourself, others, and our planet as we go through these turbulent times together.

THE PETITION

How Thought and Intention Work Together

When we think, we form an energetic cloud in space. Picture the bubble caption in a cartoon that shows what the characters are thinking or saying, and you get the general idea. If we act on our thought, the thought can be used by us or by others to create or do something.

We can intend that our thoughts be used in some constructive manner in alignment with the Creator's Will. The energetic tool we use to achieve this is an interactive request called a **Petition**. When a Petition is correctly formed, the Petition can be used in conjunction with Divine Love. Thus, the Petition should carefully define what we are trying to accomplish.

Here are two variations of a general Petition. The one immediately below is for a person doing a *specific* human healing. See Chapter 10 for more information on using the Petition.

> **"With my Soul, I accept Divine Love and surrender my will to the Creator's Will. I acknowledge my (state a health issue here) and ask that the source of this (problem) be released and corrected in my system with Divine Love according to the Creator's Will."**

The next general Petition is for all other things.

Surviving Chaos: Healing With Divine Love

"With my Soul, I accept Divine Love and surrender my will to the Creator's Will. I acknowledge <u>(state the problem here)</u> and ask that the source of this <u>(problem)</u> be released and corrected with Divine Love according to the Creator's Will."

This information is intended to show you how to *change* things in the environment and world without violating people's rights or the Creator's Will. The information is also intended to help people to awaken to their spiritual nature and to Divine Love. Using either of these comprehensive Petitions, our earlier Personal Energy Equation of: $S+DL+P+F = $ *change*, now becomes:

$$P+F = Change$$

This simplified equation works, but requires that you *focus* (that's the F in the equation) the Petition and direct it to the subject of the healing. The next chapter will explore how to focus the Petition effectively, both locally and at a distance.

Chapter 6 - FOCUS

(The **F** in your Personal Energy Equation)

This chapter is critical to your understanding. It describes how to connect with yourself or with the person or thing that you are trying to *change*.

Do you remember learning in Chapter 2 that everyone can move energy from one point to another? You can propel your Petition instantaneously to a local or distant point by **focusing** on the intended target (person, place or thing) with your Soul and Divine Love energy. "Focusing" means to concentrate intensely on the task at hand without letting your attention wander to other tasks or thoughts. In this chapter, you will learn several ways to *focus* for maximum effectiveness.

We will discuss three conditions for focusing properly: **Self Focus**, where you are applying a Petition to yourself; **Helping Another Person,** where you are supporting a recipient in his or her healing; and **Group Help,** where a group is helping to *change* a person, place, or thing.

Surviving Chaos: Healing With Divine Love

Self Focus

Suppose you want to do a self-healing. How do you connect with yourself? You know that you are going to use your Soul and Divine Love, and you may have included them by reference in your Petition.

How to connect:

> Connect yourself as the target of your Petition by drawing in and holding your breath.
>
> Tell yourself mentally to focus on your thymus with your Soul and Divine Love.
>
> Recite the Petition mentally.
>
> Slowly let your breath out.
>
> Continue to focus on your thymus for about 5 minutes.

The first time you breathe out, the Petition is energized and surrounds your body. You are literally in an energy bubble that acts on your body as long as you continue to hold *focus* in this manner. Continue to breathe slowly during the five minutes and do not let your mind wander. If it does, start over. We use the thymus because it distributes Divine Love evenly throughout the body.

You can use this method to release and correct many

emotional feelings, pains, or limitations. You can usually accomplish this in about five minutes. When the time is up, use your muscle test to see if the *change* is complete throughout your system. If it is complete, you are done and the Petition dissolves. If it is not complete, repeat the process a second time. The Petition may still be energized. However, we do not want to leave anything to chance, so *repeat the entire process.* Also continue to *focus* on your entire being with Divine Love for another five minutes. Then muscle test yourself again to see if the *change* is complete. If you do not achieve full results, ask someone to assist you.

Keep in mind that *energy follows thought*, and *Divine Love* acts on a human being to satisfy a *Petition*. If you stop focusing on your thymus, the Petition will slowly discharge, and the self-healing will come to a halt.

For some problems (such as an emotional upset, mild headache, or unwanted behavior that you are trying to *change)*, a five- to ten-minute session is all that you will need. If you do not achieve satisfactory results within ten minutes, stop the effort. Retry the healing with another person assisting you or seek group help.

To *change* a long-term illnesses, such as a life-threatening condition that does not respond to medical treatment, you will need group help. Generally, a group is needed because one or two people simply do not possess sufficient energy to make the necessary *change*. A large group usually provides excess energy over that which is needed. This excess energy concept also applies when you are trying to help one or more people simultaneously, or to *change* something in nature.

Helping Another Person (the recipient)

To help another person, hold an intention to focus on this recipient with Divine Love. Do not attempt to heal another person; that is the other person's objective, not yours. Your objective is to help the recipient to boost the level of Divine Love available to him or her while the recipient does the work using the person's self *focus* and own Petition. As before, if you don't achieve satisfactory results within ten minutes, stop the effort. Retry the healing with group help.

Group Help

A group working together to help someone, or to *change* something, can be effective at any distance. To help a human being, the group *focuses* on the target recipient with Divine Love. If the recipient is able, he or she focuses on his or her own thymus, recites his or her Petition, and receives the needed energetic help. The energy available to the recipient is the total combined Divine Love energy of the group plus the recipient. A group healing for a recipient seldom takes more that ten minutes if the group has a sufficient number of people. Usually fifteen people is enough for correcting most human ailments.

To *change* any non-human application, you will note two major differences that will be described fully in Chapter 8. First, more people may be needed in the group and second, it is the group that initiates the Petition.

With a little practice, sensitive people in the group can tell when energy is flowing properly. They can tell when the recipient has finished processing because the group energy flow will shut off abruptly once the *change* has been completed.

Breath Pulse

Many healing disciplines use a breath pulse as part of their technique. Pulsing your breath is a way of moving energy. It is a special intention to do something while you are holding a Focus.

Some people like to pulse breath to release energy in themselves, sort of like giving yourself permission to release yourself energetically from an issue. For example, if you are trying to release a problem described in a Petition, you may feel a desire to pulse your breath. Know however that when you pulse breath, the Focus on self is broken. The Petition resides for a while until it runs out of energy. Then it will collapse just like air coming out of a balloon. If you are acting alone, your connection with yourself is lost. You are better off holding a Focus on yourself for the time suggested.

Surviving Chaos: Healing With Divine Love

When you finish a group healing, it is common practice for the group to pulse breath to disengage themselves from the target.

A breath pulse is correctly achieved when you take a deep breath, close your mouth and lips and pulse out your breath lightly but suddenly, as if you were blowing your nose. Pulsing breath is also a way of releasing yourself from a Petition created for other purposes as was described in the additional skills section of Chapter 4.

Review

We started with what looked like a complex Personal Energy Equation to make *changes*. This equation consisted of Soul, Divine Love, a Petition, and a Focus on the target.

Your Personal Energy Equation from Chapter 5 was:

$$\mathbf{P + F =} \textit{ Change}$$

Now you understand the "F" and have all the pieces of your final Personal Energy Equation.

Chapter 7 - INNER WORKINGS

Petition Requests

To comprehend our interaction with a Petition, we need to understand that we are spiritual beings capable of interacting with Divine Love. If the Creator agrees with the Petition, Divine Love acts to effect *change*. If the Creator does not agree, the Petition does not get energized and does not act in whole or in part.

As you maintain proper *focus*, the Creator usually grants your Petition and Divine Love begins to instantly act upon you or the person, place, or thing that you describe. It is not hard. You have read the proofs. Try it with confidence. Your individual and group results can be profound.

Test for the completion of every *change* that you undertake. You can determine your progress and results with muscle testing, by observation, and by medical tests, if they are available.

Should you determine during muscle testing that something is not being corrected, I suggest you muscle test to find out why. Sometimes a Petition is simply not granted. Generally it is because you want something but are not willing to assume responsibility for changing your own behavior to achieve or maintain your wellness. Find out what the underlying problem is and correct that problem first with a separate Petition. After the problem has been corrected, return to your original Petition effort.

Understanding Energy Changes

The mechanism to explain what happens when sufficient energy is applied to something has been taught in science for years:

Apply the right energy and matter is disassociated, or converted to something else.

While science currently demonstrates this general principle through chemistry, nuclear physics, and quantum physics, can science explain how Petition-based spiritual energy healing works? No, it cannot.

We are left then with another reality. This reality is that there really is a Divine presence in the universe. We are all part of the Divine, even though we may not understand the inner workings. After all, how many of us can really explain how a TV works? Yet we all know how to turn it on and select channels to watch. So it is with the Petition. It is given and it works.

Are we really making the *change* ourselves? The answer is *yes* and *no*. What we are doing is *asking through our Soul* that the right action be taken to make a *change. It is Divine Love that does the work and makes the spiritual, mental, and physical changes happen, not you or me.*

People who study energy healing frequently miss the point of successful healing. That point is:

**Without a belief in and reverence
for the Creator and Divine Love,
a Petition is not granted.**

Here is another way of looking at these healing principles. The Creator has given us a toolkit to use if we want to use it. It is up to us to do something for ourselves. It's like any competitive sport. We must do something on our own, or we will get overrun by the opposition if we are foolish enough to just stand still on the playing field.

Some people may argue that we are interfering with the Divine. We see that as uninformed. Rather, the Creator allows us to do whatever we want. The wiser approach is to operate within the Creator's Will. Then if the Creator grants a Petition to heal or to restore our planet, *change* occurs because the Creator has given us that permission.

Surviving Chaos: Healing With Divine Love

Choices

We all have a choice. We can sit idly by while other people plunder the human race and destroy the earth. Or we can interact in a loving and proactive manner with the Creator to *change* the outcomes for the present and future.

Everything is energy. Bad intentions and the number of people exhibiting self-serving objectives may outnumber those people whose intentions are for the higher good. However, people serving the higher good will prevail on earth if they use the tenets of Divine Love properly. That is, Divine Love is the most powerful force in the universe that enables a petitioner to initiate *changes*.

A Worldwide Problem: The Unconsciousness of People

We need to agree on what is meant by "unconsciousness" so we are all on the same page in what we do. Consciousness is an energetic phenomenon. We can identify two states of consciousness: *sleeping* consciousness and *awake* consciousness.

A *sleeping* consciousness may see the world as a playground, where human rights, Divinity, and respect for life are not necessarily priorities. An individual living in a *sleeping* consciousness tends to operate on a basis where the end justifies the means and the person does not recognize his or her true spiritual nature. This person is called *sleeping* because he or she is not in balance with his or her Soul and is not living a Spirit-directed life. We can add to this definition, but you have the basic idea.

Over time *sleeping* consciousness has led to behavior based upon personal power and materialism. A *sleeping* consciousness accounts for many of the present conditions we see around the world in how people identify and solve, or do not solve, key problems that threaten human existence.

An *awake* consciousness is typified by the a view that *all mankind is seen as spiritual beings with Souls, rather than simply material bodies seeking spiritual meaning.* Living a spiritually directed life based upon spiritual truth, rightness, and alignment with the Creator are the most important objectives of an *awake* consciousness.

Review

As individual consciousness awakens, it sees how man has polluted, destroyed, and exploited the planet. We can ask that Divine Love restore, alter, or repair current problems and affect future outcomes consistent with the Creator's Will via our Petitions. The next chapter describes how we can do this.

"The less we look
with our eyes, the
more we will see with
our hearts."

Lyndsey Albrecht

"When one door
closes another door
opens; but we so
often look so long and
so regretfully upon
the closed door, that
we do not see the
ones which open for
us."

Helen Keller

Chapter 8 - APPLICATIONS

Personal Alignment

You can align yourself spiritually with the Creator regardless of your past actions or your belief systems. Changes may be coming that may cause you mental and physical pain unless you accept personal responsibility for yourself and are prepared to help yourself. The last chapter discussed unconsciousness and simplified the explanation purposely. Hopefully, you will take action to become *awake* in consciousness if you are not already in that state.

Spiritual truth is the key to survival and defines all things that the Creator would prefer us to follow in order to be in harmony and peace with Divine Intelligence. Throughout history, many world teachers have said essentially the same thing in various ways. They offered guidance on how to achieve oneness with the Creator. Despite the massive forward strides our civilization has made, we have not implemented this spiritual teaching very well. We continue to be distracted by physical gain rather than spiritual alignment.

The Introduction identified future possibilities. We do

not know the Creator's will or timetable for any possible future occurrence. However, you now have tools that you can use should any of these things happen—even if you find you are on your own because services of all kinds become severely limited.

You can customize a Petition to suit yourself and it will be effective—provided that you remember to include the components of your original Personal Energy Equation.

Importance of Self-Clearing

This chapter contains information that is new for most readers. I suggest that you start by using your Personal Energy Equation to conduct a self-clearing so that you may discern the spiritual truth. Try a Petition like this one:

> **With my Soul, I accept Divine Love. I surrender my total self—Soul, Mind, and Body —to the Creator's will. I desire to release everything in me that is spiritually and mentally untrue and to have that knowledge replaced in me by spiritual truth according to the Creator's will.**

Now let's get down to the purpose of this book—learning to make energetic changes that can result in physical change.

Changes

In this section, you will find that you can best attain *change* through large-group participation. One of the spiritual teachings that man has yet to fully learn is to spiritually love and help one another. Consequently, a group healing is often the vehicle that the Creator uses to teach us love.

With group healings, only one person in the group needs to state the Petition. The other participants hold a focus of Divine Love on the target before, during, and after the Petition is spoken.

Pollution Correction

Maintaining an adequate supply of potable water is a worldwide problem right now. Much of our water is contaminated by radiation particles, chemicals, bacteria, and viruses.

In energy healing work, the method of purifying water takes an energetic form that you may not be expecting. When you use a Petition to make polluted water potable, applying the Divine Love energy to the water provides energetic protection. You can then consume the water without experiencing adverse effects. This may sound like a tall tale, but consider the following story.

In October 2008, the National Geographic Channel's

episode of *Taboo* showed a group of Asian healer trainees grinding up fluorescent light tubes. The tubes were coated inside with a compound of powdered mercury—a deadly poison. The trainees were able to chew and swallow the glass and made a point of rubbing their fingers in the mercury compound and then eating the compound as well. They are unaffected by the glass or poison because they operate with the knowledge that Divine Love protects them.

You can achieve similar results with contaminated water using a Petition asking to **make the contaminated water safe to use and consume**. After healing the water, do a Self-Truth test to ensure that the water is now safe to drink. Remember, your body doesn't lie. If the water still isn't safe, add people to your group and try the Petition again, holding *focus* longer. Be sure to consume only water that tests safe.

Plant Growth

Plants grow better if you first apply a Petition to the water you give them. Such a Petition could be to **grow the plants faster and provide necessary plant nutrition**.

Not only do the plants grow rapidly, *but they also require far less water* and produce abundantly. Perform this service when the seeds are first planted as well as throughout the growing season.

Food Contaminants

Food contamination from bacteria, radiation and chemicals has been on the rise in the last few years. This contamination can be from:

- contaminated water used on crops
- chemicals absorbed by the plant roots or leaves
- unsanitary handling, refrigeration, storage, or shipping
- contaminated feed that animals have eaten
- nuclear contamination

Before you consume food, use a Petition to **clear any contamination from the food and make it safe to eat.** You can also do this to prevent food from spoiling if refrigeration is unavailable. Again, be sure to muscle test that the food is safe before you or your family consume it.

Nuclear Radiation Poisoning

The radiation effect from low-level radioactive ammunition made from spent uranium has become yet another health concern. When a spent uranium projectile impacts a target, radioactive particles scatter, and then troops and other people in the war zone ingest them in one way or another. The more exploded shells there are, the more radioactive particle exposure people receive. The result can be horrific sores, birth defects, cancers, breathing problems, and ultimately death. Similar symptoms can develop from a nuclear explosion when people are within the radiation field emitted from a bomb.

People can also be contaminated by airborne radiation particles from any source, including radon (a low-level radioactive gas) seeping into a home from the earth.

Land Healing

Radioactive land should be healed because radioactive particles can remain in the soil for hundreds of years, polluting livestock, people, water, and plants for generations to come. The concentration of radiation in soil varies, depending upon the situation.

Radiation Healing

As you would expect, the amount of human radiation exposure and the resulting cell damage varies based upon the severity of the exposure. As a result, it's usually not possible to determine beforehand how many people are needed in a group to help a person poisoned by radiation. You could start with say, a hundred people, but that may be too many or too few. Since your cells do not have the knowledge concerning exact group size, muscle testing is not the answer.

Furthermore, you may have only a few people

available to help, which may not be enough to supply the energy that's needed. (Think of how ineffective a candle flame is that is trying to melt an iceberg.) So, what can you do to help?

The answer lies in modifying the Petition, because the good news is that we are not limited. Under unusual circumstances, you can construct a Petition for your group to be enabled with sufficient Divine Love energy to complete the healing work on whatever people, places, or things you set out to heal! Granting this special Petition is up to the Creator. If it were granted, each member of your group would be temporarily enabled to raise his or her energy level high enough to accomplish the group's objective. This would happen only if each person's system was able to handle the energy and if you have sufficient group energy to do the job.

I suggest a beginning group size of 50 people acting together at the same time. Your Petition might look like this:

> **With our Souls, we accept Divine Love. We surrender our will to the Creator's will. We acknowledge the radiation damage in (name the person, people, animals, or land) and ask that the Creator provide within us sufficient Divine Love energy to render this radiation harmless and to heal the damage, in accordance with the Creator's will.**

Surviving Chaos: Healing With Divine Love

One person can state the Petition, but everyone in the group should hear that person's words as each of them focuses on the target with Divine Love. The group should hold its focus for ten minutes and then stop to confirm success by asking through muscle testing what percent of the target is now complete. If you are making sufficient progress with the group, repeat the Petition. Otherwise, increase group size and try again.

You can also hold a sample of food, earth, plants, or water in your hand and do a test for safe consumption or for rendering the radiation harmless. This works because the sample energy is part of your energy when you hold it.

How do you determine that a radiation-damaged person, who is at a distance, is completely healed? Your own body does not have cellular knowledge about someone else's body. In this case, you must turn the problem around! You become a spiritual proxy for the ill person by aligning with them on a spiritual basis. Then, you can test the person's system for them by acting as that person.

To be a proxy, state to yourself that you are acting on behalf of <u>(name the person)</u> and perform your muscle test. Then you can ask muscle testing questions to test for percent complete. If necessary resume the group healing effort. After the healing, test again to ensure that the healing is complete throughout both the energetic and the physical systems of the target. If the proxy muscle test indicates that the target is not completely healed, repeat the healing for ten more minutes and/or add more people to your group and try again.

When this activity is complete, remember to tell yourself that you are no longer a proxy for that person and that you are now operating fully as yourself.

Hysteria and Disturbed Behavior

Crowds tend to react in the same manner when disaster strikes. Wherever you encounter widespread panic and desperate behavior driven by emotion, use a Petition to ask to **restore mental balance and peace in all the people located at (name the place).** You will find that the people will quickly return to a calm state.

As laymen, none of us are qualified to diagnose the mental condition of anyone else. However, at times it becomes obvious that balance is needed, especially when behavior becomes extreme (as in a person hurting other people). In these cases, use a Petition to ask to **restore mental balance and rational thought in (name the people or place).**

Many people lack a basic understanding of love. They do not feel human love, let alone spiritual love. To help these people, you can use a Petition to **release all false beliefs about love and enable (person's**

name) to understand spiritual truth and spiritual love.

Group Think

We have a massive international problem today because many groups with special interests have adopted limited thought processes that favor their beliefs and desires. They seem reluctant to change or negotiate unless a proposed change supports their position.

We can deal with most such problems by changing the group-think limitations of the population using a simple Petition. This Petition might include a request to **convert all that is wrong in the thinking and actions of our people to that which is spiritually and physically right and true for all people**. Take care that you not try to manipulate the situation in any specific way other than to provide help based upon the spiritual truth and not on our limited belief. If you try to use this Petition to accomplish your own purposes rather than the Creator's, the Petition will not work because it will have no energy behind it.

Review

I mentioned up front that this would be a book that would open your eyes to what can be. Now you know that every person can apply his or her Personal Energy Equation to help just about any situation.

Purifying drinking water may take one or more people.

Complex human healings may take 15 people acting together in a group to help a single recipient.

For larger problems, such as radiation events, you will need to apply even more energy quickly to reduce suffering. You can do this by constructing a Petition that your group members be enabled to access whatever level of Divine Love is needed for complete healing.

Cautions

Results are not assured, as they depend on your spiritual belief in what you do with a Petition as well as on what the Creator is willing to grant.

Don't waste your time trying to manipulate a situation or people to fit your agenda. That will simply not work.

Your best intentions to correct something very broad (like the entire unconsciousness of every human being in the world), while admirable, is subject to the Creator's will.

Humanity can become aligned with the Creator's Spirit right now, and we can act as spiritual human beings to make the world a better place.

Surviving Chaos: Healing With Divine Love

Use your Personal Energy Equation—particularly if you are in a life-threatening situation. Be observant and watch for *change*, validating results with muscle testing. When possible, follow up with medical testing.

When I began healing work in 1980, I had a very limited exposure to unseen energy. I had to build a foundation on what I knew to be true. My motto was:

> The truth is what you can make happen.

Over the years, I learned that my original motto should have been:

> The truth is what you can make happen with the Creator's support.

"The greatest conflicts are not between two people, but between one person and himself."

Garth Brooks

Chapter 9 - SOUL AND SPIRIT

Up to this point, you have read about using the Soul in your Personal Energy Equation. My current research and healing work is based exclusively upon using Soul in a Petition.

At this point, I am going to examine a subtle change that is happening on earth. Starting in August 2008, people started contacting me to report *sudden* and *debilitating* pain that would occur in knees, joints, chests, necks, and limbs for no obvious reason. My best efforts to help them using a Soul-based Petition were ineffective. Nothing happened!

This motivated me to determine what was going on in their systems. I did this sensing through intuition, and I confirmed the results by doing proxy muscle testing, as well as having my clients do their own independent muscle testing. I asked them to test to see if the Creator's Spirit energy was trying to replace Soul energy in their bodies.

What we determined has staggering implications that I would like to share with you.

Surviving Chaos: Healing With Divine Love

First, let me explain a key point. The Soul, the Mind, and the Body can contain energy disturbances that can interfere with healing. When we use Soul in a Petition, most of the problems that concern us are corrected according to the will of the Creator. Yet I've also had clients whose Soul itself had a disturbance that did not and would not correct. For many years, some energy healers believed that certain recipients could not be helped. These healers did not understand that the Soul of the recipient was resisting a change.

What We Discovered

Some people are experiencing a conversion from operating as a *soul-based* human being to operating as a *spirit-based* human being. These people operate under the guidance of their Spirit rather than of their Soul. This is important because Spirit is already correctly aligned with the Creator's energy. Furthermore, Spirit cleanses Soul interference.

When I had these clients substitute *Spirit* for *Soul* in a custom-worded Petition that asked for a Spirit-guided existence from the Creator, most conditions cleared up within days. Each Recipient initiated this higher connection to the Creator.

I believe the rapid clearing happened because the Spirit is pure and reflects more clearly the will of the Creator, whereas the Soul can carry old baggage.

Some of you have read about or have already experienced this transition using the term the "Holy Spirit." The higher dimension of Spirit is a higher vibration than Soul. Corrections in energy disturbances flow from Spirit to Soul to Mind and finally to Body at a rate that human beings can energetically handle.

What Does This Transition Mean To Mankind?

I do not take sides, yet I think that the implications are pretty clear. Intuitive people and ancient-world prophets have forecast major earth changes accruing over a seven-year period ending somewhere between 2010 and 2012. Some refer to this as the "End Times." Others believe that the universe will experience an electromagnetic shift that may introduce unwanted changes like earth magnetic pole shifts, global warming, severe storms, and solar radiation that has the potential to adversely affect all of us!

This book is concerned with addressing and solving broad world-wide problems that are beginning to happen *now*. Within these pages, I have detailed what you can do to help by using spiritual energy healing techniques while working in a group.

In the case of exposure to either solar or nuclear radiation, this book suggests an approximate number of people required to do a Soul-based healing. The practical question is how long do we have to wait to observe physical results? Recall that each person in a group can project his or her own energy level of Divine Love. Therefore, a group must access the right amount and level of Divine Love to make *change* happen.

Since Divine Love makes the *change*, it follows that the more people there are in a group, the more energy the group can bring to bear on a problem. It's important to understand and access the level of Divine Love energy that is needed in various group mixes of Spirit-based and Soul-based members.

If the healing situation requires a very high level of Divine Love, some of the group members may not be given access to the energy level needed. That is to protect them from energy overload. (A good example of this would be when a sudden energy influx overwhelms a recipient and knocks the person down.) The remedy is to add more people to the group until the group can deal effectively with the problem.

If the group were composed of only Soul-based people, it might take a long time (perhaps weeks) to achieve *change* in a large problem.

Conversely, Spirit-based people already operate at the same high-energy level. Therefore, they can handle most complex problems by adding the right number of Spirit-based people to any group.

Radiation correction is a special case. We can measure radiation in various ways using detectors to report the cumulative exposure in human beings. If the subject receives more than the allowable radiation limit, cell mutation follows. Nuclear radiation exists for various time intervals, depending upon the type of radioactive elements that were used initially. Tests measure how long it takes for a radioactive particle to decay to zero radiation. This decay can be hours, months, or *hundreds of years*.

Since each member of a Spirit-based group can handle the same level of Divine Love energy, I suggest that these people use a single comprehensive Petition to correct a particular radiation incident in the people, animals, water, food, and so on in a given location.

With groups composed of mostly Soul-based people, I suggest breaking the problem down into smaller components. Use one Petition for people, another Petition for animals, a third Petition for land, a fourth for water, and so forth.

A Special Petition

Based upon my observation, many people are moving from Soul to Spirit without being aware of it (as was the case with the clients I described earlier in this chapter). I suggest that you try the Soul-to-Spirit Petition provided below to fully awaken spiritually so that you may then help yourself, your families, and others more effectively.

Surviving Chaos: Healing With Divine Love

With my *Soul* I focus the energy of Divine Love into my thymus. I surrender my will to the Creator's will. I acknowledge all my pain and I ask that my system receive my *Spirit* fully and that it correct all these conditions according to Divine will.

Do not despair if you do not transform from a Soul-based to a Spirit-based life. This simply means that the Creator's plan for your life does not require this transformation. It is not a reward or a punishment. It simply is!

You can use your muscle test to check the percent completion of your transition. Once your transition is complete, you can also muscle test for spiritual gifts that the Creator has given to you, such as increased intuition.

You can create a muscle test scale from 0 (meaning not important to you) to 1000 (representing total spiritual and physical Truth and being very important to you). Use the scale to set priorities for *change*.

Once you have successfully completed the Soul-to-Spirit Petition, you will be operating as a Spirit-based person. From this point on, you will want to use Spirit when you make a Petition. Here is a sample Petition to use after making the transition to a Spirit-based person for anything in your own life that you want to *change*:

Using my *Spirit*, I focus the energy of Divine Love into my problem area. I surrender my will to the Creator's will. I acknowledge my (state your personal problem) and release it and whatever causes it to the Creator. I ask that my system be corrected according to the Creator's will.

Remember to maintain *focus* throughout. You will quickly observe that you can then release and self-correct many issues in yourself that you could not do as a Soul-based human being without the support of a group.

Effectiveness In Healing

I realize that this chapter contains the most involved concepts in this book, so here are two tables designed to help your understanding. They show the various principles this chapter has just presented.

The Tables assume that:

> 1. A *target* is the person, place, or thing that is receiving healing energy.

> 2. The healers and the targets (if human) believe in the Creator and in Divine Love.

I use an "X" to denote the energy equivalents of Divine Love that a group can access using various numbers of people.

Table 1: Soul-Based vs. Spirit-Based Effectiveness

If the Healer is:	Target is:	Petition results:
One Soul-based person	Self	a. Energy level is 1X. b. Rapid results for emotional issues. c. Does not generate enough energy to correct illness in reasonable time.
One Soul-based person	Another Soul-based person	a. Energy level is 2X. b. May still not generate sufficient energy to correct major illness.
15 Soul-based people in a group	One Soul-based person	a. Energy level is 16X. b. Energy high enough to correct most non-radiation illness.
One Spirit-based person	Self	Acting alone, can correct illness in self in reasonable time, including radiation events.
4 Spirit-based people	Solving world-wide problems involving persons, places, or things	a. Energy input is 4X but is a much higher energy than an equivalent 4X in a Soul-based group. b. Shorter time for a *change*. c. Requires fewer people to *change* large-scale problems.

Do not think of Table 1 as a requirement to change from what you comfortably do right now. Some people may operate at much higher levels of energy than you; and some operate at lower levels. This is a normal occurrence. As your system clears itself from a lifetime of disinformation and illness, your energy level will increase.

Table 2: Energy Transfer Dynamics

Using a Soul-based group, sized to meet a target need.	a. Completes *change* in about 10 minutes for non-radiation healing. b. Can size group to handle radiation, but requires many people and *focus* time varies with level of radiation. c. Divine Love acts immediately on target.
Using a Spirit-based group, sized to meet a target need.	a. Completes *change* in about 5 minutes for most healing. b. Requires fewer people than Soul-based group but does need to be sized to produce *change* in reasonable time. c. Divine Love acts immediately on target.

In all healing efforts, whether Soul-based or Spirit-based, if you do not attain any results in five to ten minutes, stop your activity. Have a member of the group use muscle testing or intuition to determine what the group should do next. Then make the necessary adjustments and repeat the Petition.

"Do everything with so much love in your heart that you would never want to do it any other way."

Yogi Desai

"The World is not dangerous because of those who do harm, but because of those who look at it without doing anything."

Albert Einstein

Chapter 10 - TRAINING COURSE
Section 1

Introduction

DLGHP is the abbreviation for the Divine Love Group Healing Process. Thousands of people have been exposed to this self-teaching course since it was made available to the public. The DLGHP is the basic technique that has enabled us to pursue the unusual application solutions described in Chapter 8.

The Program is divided into two Sections for your use and study.

Section 1 again explains the Process and how to use it. **Chapter 11 Section 2** offers background on energy of various types and human response to energy. I suggest you go through this self-teaching course at least once if you are interested in getting more in-information on energy principles and energy healing.

Group Healing has been around a long time with varying degrees of success. The DLGHP herein called the "**Process**" is different for seven reasons:

1. The Process uses Divine Love, a time-tested

Petition, plus an activation procedure that is used to effect spiritual based healing involving the Creator.

2. The Petition is carefully composed and designed to serve most healing situations.

3. There are three Process healing formats from which to select.

4. The Process can be learned and applied in a matter of minutes, once you understand the principles.

5. The Process is the result of years of fine-tuning to gain a proper understanding that could be explained in this teaching course.

6. Emotional, mental and physical problem solutions are addressed.

7. Multiple people can be served simultaneously.

Energy Transfer Principles

All matter is held together by oscillating energy fields. When these fields are correctly stimulated, change occurs in matter. Science is pursuing stimulation of matter through particle physics. The Process achieves the same result using spiritual energy. See Chapter 11 for more background.

In Chapter 2 I covered the proofs conducted in scientific laboratory experiments that revealed a fundamental truth about people: *Human beings can transmit energy, just like a radio or television.* Further, I learned through trial and error that when we correctly transmit an intention of loving service to someone in need, healing energy flows to that person.

And finally as I learned to help people release emotional, mental and physical problems with Divine Love, I observed that people's health improved.

Definition Of Divine Love

How would you go about defining the term Divine Love?

If you have a religious belief system, you probably know that almost every religion in the world has a spiritual history that teaches that man is derived from a spiritual being. We will call that being, the *Creator.* You can freely substitute the name of the being that you worship.

Whatever your belief, realize that all healing comes through the Creator's continuous love for us. We humans can be conduits of His love as we strive to honor the Creator, nature and mankind. Think of Divine Love as the glue that binds us together. The Creator's love is Divine Love.

Surviving Chaos: Healing With Divine Love

How We Experience Divine Love

Have you ever watched an ice cream cone melting on a hot day? The ice cream gets soft and sort of oozes down the cone, doesn't it? Did you know that Divine Love can "melt away" health problems that cause un-wellness? These problems can be safely corrected with the Process without exposing anyone to unpleas-antness, such as reliving a tragedy, trauma, or other incident. Results are usually profound and achievable within a short time.

You need to know that:

    1. The success of your healing lies in your willing-ness to accept Divine Love within yourself.

    2. Divine Love is available to all of us. It does not matter where you come from, whether or not you have an education or wealth, what nationality you claim, your age, sex, politics, or religion.

    3. This form of healing is *not* charismatic or faith healing, nor can any religious group claim ownership.

    4. Many emotional and health difficulties can be permanently removed very quickly with the Process.

    5. ***The Process works!*** I know this is true be-cause I have watched people recover from debilitating health problems by using the Process where no other solution worked.

Where To Use The DLGHP

The Process can be used anywhere at any time, but I suggest you experience it in a safe, quiet environment where you are not operating machinery, watching TV or distracted by children, people, animals or sounds.

The DLGHP

We refer to the person receiving a healing as a *Recipient* to make this training course clear. In what follows, the Recipient uses his thymus gland as a point of contact with his body. I have found that this is very effective. The thymus is located about an inch below the juncture of the two collar bones, behind the sternum.

There are three Process formats that can be experienced: Unassisted, Assisted and Large Group Healing. Detailed instruction for each format will be given later in this course. Here is a summary of the three formats:

Unassisted: A Recipient initiates the Process through the thymus with Divine Love and recites the Petition aloud. The Recipient sits quietly, breathes slowly and deeply for several minutes while concentrating on the thymus. If satisfactory results are not achieved within ten minutes, attend a Large Group Healing.

Surviving Chaos: Healing With Divine Love

Assisted: A spiritual friend or health care practitioner focuses with Divine Love on a Recipient. The Recipient initiates the Process. The Recipient sits quietly, breathes slowly and deeply for several minutes concentrating on the thymus while the spiritual friend continues to transmit an intention of Divine Love to the Recipient. If the two people working together do not produce the desired results, attend a Large Group Healing.

Large Group Healing: A Group of ten or more spiritual people can work together to assist one Recipient. I suggest a Group size of 15 for difficult illnesses that do not respond to conventional medical treatment or where multiple Recipients are being simultaneously served.

As before, the Group focuses on transmitting Divine Love to the Recipient(s). The Recipient(s) initiate the Process. The Group holds their focus on the Recipient(s). Each Recipient stays focused on his/her own thymus until the Group determines that the Process is complete.

Please remember: Some people will heal faster and some slower, according to the Will of the Creator and the ability of the Recipient's system to process energy as the healing proceeds.

The Petition

> **"I accept Divine Love and surrender my will to the Creator's Will. I acknowledge my (name the symptoms), and ask that the source of this problem be released and corrected in my system with Divine Love according to the Creator's Will."**

Many people want to know what the words mean as they use the Petition. When a Recipient says, " I accept Divine Love and surrender my will to the Creator's Will", the Recipient is giving himself permission to take in the Creator's Divine Love and align and subjugate the Recipient's will to the Creator's Will. This is important because the Creator is in charge of what happens, not the Recipient and not a Group.

When the Recipient says," I acknowledge my" the Recipient is admitting via the symptom that there is something amiss in the Recipient's body that needs correction. This could be a mental issue as well.

When the Recipient says, "and ask that the source of this problem be released and corrected in my system with Divine Love", the Recipient is giving himself permission to surrender the problem source to the Creator and agreeing to the correction in the Recipient's system.

And finally, when the Recipient says "according to the Creator's Will", the Recipient is accepting the

Creator's plan for the Recipient, rather than willfully trying to force a healing to meet Recipient or Group desires.

Group Mechanics

Meaning And Use Of Focus

This term applies to both a Recipient and the Group. To "focus" means to concentrate one's attention somewhere or upon something and not be distracted by other thoughts, actions, or conversations. One might stare at another person, but this makes people feel uncomfortable. A softer approach is to close your eyes and simply concentrate as if you were solving a problem where you are thinking intently.

Group Action

Each member of the Group "focuses" on a Recipient by drawing in breath, holding the intention of "sending (transmitting) Divine Love to the Recipient" and slowly releasing breath toward the Recipient. Then the Group continues to sit quietly holding their focus on the Recipient without conversation or distractions until the Process is complete - usually less than ten minutes.

Recipient Action

This is how a Recipient initiates the Process:

     1. Following the Group Action, draw in breath and hold the intention of "sending Divine Love directly into my thymus", then release breath slowly.

     2. Recite the Petition aloud. Sit quietly for about ten minutes while the Spiritual Healing proceeds until the Recipient does not feel further energy movement in his body (if the Recipient is acting alone), or the Group tells the Recipient to stop.

Importance Of Deep Breathing

I have learned that proper deep breathing helps a Recipient facilitate the healing Process by increasing the oxygen intake of his/her bloodstream. Proper breathing is an optional part of the Process. It can be done by a Recipient during the Process to keep his/her attention focused on the Process. Recipients report that deep breathing for about ten minutes leaves them feeling fully energized.

A 4-cycle breathing method is helpful after a Recipient has gone home should the Recipient feel any fatigue.

Correct breathing is done in four cycles:

Surviving Chaos: Healing With Divine Love

1. Take a slow deep breath.

2. Hold your breath about two or three seconds.

3. Breathe out slowly and completely. Empty your lungs.

4. Don't breathe in for two or three seconds, then repeat breathing cycle 1-4.

Please remember to breathe very slowly and deeply so that you do not get light-headed or hyperventilate. If you do get" fuzzy" simply breathe in deeply and hold your breath for ten seconds. Then resume the four-cycle breathing.

Using The Correct Process Format

Divine Love healing energy increases as people are added to the Group. When experiencing the **Unassisted** format a Recipient may not always bring sufficient energy to bear on his problem.

If results are not forthcoming, seek a **Large Group** to attain higher energy and maximum *change*. A single emotional problem will usually be dissolved in minutes, leaving a person in a state of well-being, together with the potential release of local aches and pains. Either the **Unassisted** or **Assisted** format can be used.

A medically diagnosed psychiatric condition should be handled in the presence of a trained therapist. Use the **Assisted** format.

Advanced bodily diseases are addressed only in a **Large Group Healing** format. Here the healing effort by the Group may optionally extend to twenty minutes, but not more. A Recipient should wait about ten days, to assure that the spiritual healing process is complete, then verify results with medical tests.

Some conditions are not meant to be healed. If a Recipient does not show any progress after ten days, do not do a second Large Group healing because the healing is not meant to be.

Recipient and Group Dynamics

There are twelve important dynamics regarding Groups and Recipients.

1. When a Recipient first initiates the Process, the Recipient or the Group may feel energetic effects that slowly subside and stop. This can be the sensation of heat, vibration, tingling, color, or fleeting images. It is also possible that no one feels anything. You generally stop the healing session based upon intuition.

2. The Group should be composed of people who are in reasonably good spiritual, mental and physical condition.

3. With a Group size of 15 or more, multiple Recipients can be simultaneously served, provided that the Petition is the same for all the Recipients. In this case it is more effective to have a Group Leader lead the Recipients in reciting the Petition in phrases. Each Recipient repeats the Petition phrases aloud and in unison, as would be done in a complex swearing in ceremony.

4. Recipients should be separated approximately ten feet from each other to avoid interference from each other's energy fields. Group members can sit anywhere but should be separated from Recipients by about ten feet as well.

5. A Recipient should *not* be a member of a Group for ten or more days following the Recipient's healing session because it may put strain on the Recipient's body.

6. We tried Group work where everyone in the Group was a Recipient; the Process was less effective.

7. We also tested the condition where the Group was composed of mostly ill people. This situation is also to be avoided as the Group energy generated is generally too low to be effective in helping a Recipient.

8. Some healing corrections require a large amount of energy that a small group may not be able to generate. If you are not getting good results, add

more healthy people to your group. Again, we have found that 10 to 15 people can usually handle most healing situations.

9. In small groups the communication can be handled informally, but in a Large Group we suggest that one person be designated Group Leader. The Leader's job is to help verbalize the Petition and determine when the Group healing is done. A sensitive person can tell when energy stops flowing; otherwise use 10 minutes for Large Group sessions for emotional problems and 20 minutes for physical disorders.

10. If a Recipient is very ill, we suggest that *only* that illness be worked upon. Additional Group healing may be needed if the Group energy is not high enough to affect desired c*hange*.

11. Before the Group goes home, I suggest that all thank the Creator for being allowed to serve their fellow man. It is through the Creator's Divine Love that we are all made well.

12. Again, I do not spend time analyzing cause and effect in illness, nor do I recommend any treatments or medications. We simply work together to

remove energy problems based upon stated symptoms, gently and quickly without experiencing painful memories or embarrassment. Do not bother to second guess what these problems are by name. If it

107

is important for you to know what they are, you will know.

Importance Of *Processing Time* In The Body

Did you know that every body is unique and needs processing time in order for it to become well? Processing time is the physical clock time that it takes for an energetic healing change to become effective in a Recipient's total being.

Recipients process healing energy at different rates. Thus, the time required for a given emotional or health problem to be processed must be determined from observation and verbal feedback from a Recipient or Group. If multiple Recipients are going through a simultaneous healing, the Group continues until Recipients have stopped processing.

There are two components of *processing time*:

1. The time spent by a Group serving a Recipient.

2. The minutes, hours or days following the Group Healing where the changes complete in the Recipient without Group involvement.

DLGHP Insights

These insights will help you to understand the

Process better.

1. The Process may or may not produce immediate results in a Recipient working alone. If a Recipient experiencing the Unassisted format does not attain results and can not get to a Large Group, then modify the problem statement (I acknowledge my...) in the Petition and go through the following list of potential problems one at a time because they may have limited your results:

Loving the Creator
Receiving the Creator's love for you
Loving yourself
Receiving love from others
Totally loving others
Forgiving yourself and others

This list can be done in one day. Wait three days and retry the Recipient's original problem statement.

2. If you are a generally well Recipient, the healing moves along very smoothly. If you are generally unwell, your body will proceed to heal at its own pace despite attempts to hasten the Process. In this case adding more than 15 people to the healing Group does not help healing.

3. Recipients often have a tendency to overdo the healing Process. Their idea is that if healing work shows results, then forcing oneself to go at a more rapid pace by closely spaced repeat healings will pro-

mote more rapid recovery. Such is generally not the case because the body can not always keep up with the physical desires of the individual. Remember these two points:

A. Work in a Group because the higher Group energy will help to complete the healing Process sooner.

B. If as a Recipient, you do not experience improvement during a healing session, rely on your inner guidance system – your intuition. If it is time to stop, then stop. Go to another Group meeting at a later date.

4. Completion of a Recipient healing in one session is controlled by the Recipient's system and Divine Will and not by the Group.

5. As a Recipient's body heals during a Group healing, the energy flow may start and stop during the healing to keep that Recipient's body in balance. The Group cannot overload the Recipient energy-wise because the Recipient's body draws exactly the amount of energy that it needs.

6. If you are the Recipient of a Group healing for a disease, wait at least 10 days and confirm your status with medical testing.

Life Problems

Here is a checklist of personal problems that you might go through. Do only the ones that apply to you. And do only one problem every two days because the problem may have a greater effect upon you than you realize. Release any problem associated with:

> Struggling to find the right job
> Holding on to old ways of doing things that did not work
> Trying to control
> Holding on to the past and avoiding change
> Being distrustful of people
> Revenge

Happily, when most people address these personal problems, they notice positive health changes. The reason for your current discomfort may be among them. Healing is a wonderful experience. Try to enjoy yourself. Remember that any energy trapped in your body can cause health problems.

Wait several days after experiencing the DLGHP before attempting further releases. Then in the comfort of your home you should be able to smoothly release these additional problems by yourself. (Do only one release a day; wait two days between self-healing releases.)

Fear	Anger	Confusion
Stress	Aloneness	Being unloved

Surviving Chaos: Healing With Divine Love

Hatred	Distrust	Depression
Guilt	Betrayal	Being rejected
Rage	Jealousy	Being abandoned
Abuse	Anxiety	Being victimized
Grief	Frustration	

Again: do no more than one of these every second day if you are acting alone.

Healing Successes

There are no guarantees or claims being made for this course, but know that many people can and have recovered from debilitating illness using this spiritual healing DLGHP. Following is a list of illnesses that from which people have recovered.

Trauma	Nerve disorders
Eating disorders	Toxins
Allergies	Cancer
Adhesions	Bone healing
Tuberculosis	Viruses
Stroke	Substance abuse
Foreign bacteria	Heart disease
Chemical poisoning	Blood diseases
Radiation damage	Sight problems
Stress	Hearing
Organ healings	Paralysis
Sexually transmitted diseases	

If you are comfortable with the principles now, you are ready to proceed because you know that you can not do anything harmful to yourself or others. And if there is no harm, you do not have to worry about what happens, or doesn't happen as you go through this Process.

The key teaching is to understand that the Creator has a complete love for all of us. The Creator's Divine Love guides our thinking to a point of extreme clarity where we eventually realize that only through the use of Divine Love can we, or the world, change for the better.

For more information on subtle energy and the use of Divine Love please review Chapter 11.

All parties must agree, prior to use, to defend and hold harmless Robert G. Fritchie and/or World Service Institute and its officers and employees from all claims against use, results, and other applications of The Divine Love Group Healing Process.

There are no guarantees for Recipient or Group healing results.

"Out of intense complexities, intense simplicities emerge."

Winston Churchill

"If you have knowledge, let others light their candles in it."

Margaret Fuller

Chapter 11- TRAINING COURSE
Section 2

This Chapter begins with a thumbnail sketch on how others look at energy and its use in healing. This is followed by some material to give you insight into how this Process and the Petition evolved over several years. It also shows why we eventually converted from using variable definitions of Spiritual Love to using Divine Love in all that we do.

As our approach to Group healing evolved, I taught many workshops before the Petition was developed. I tried to give people a nontechnical explanation of energy effects using descriptors and word pictures such as *spears, shields and programs* to make a point. I left these concepts in this Section to make it easier to understand a very complex subject.

I dropped any effort to continue using these descriptors in the Divine Love Group Healing Process given in Chapter 10. We settled on more simple terms, *symptoms*, experienced by a Recipient and used in the Petition statement of the problem. This was found adequate because Divine Love *melts* all the *spears, shields and programs* as a Large Group Healing session progresses.

Surviving Chaos: Healing With Divine Love

An Overview Of The Healing Process

Historically, references to healing were viewed as miraculous by the public because healing was simply not understood. Today we have a better understanding that allows us to explain what is happening.

Energy healers use a Universal Life Force energy. Some Spiritual Healers call this same universal life force *love energy*.

The cultures of other countries, particularly in Asia, have recognized healing effects for centuries. For example, the Chinese describe the shift from good to poor health as the human body going out of balance. Chinese medicine is dedicated to restoring the "out of balance" condition so that the body regains proper energy flow.

In recent times, researchers in Russia, Europe and the United States have studied a fairly new principle to explain illness. The principle is to consider the human body as a mixture of electric and electromagnetic fields. These fields have collectively been called bio-energy fields. The fields oscillate like an electric circuit until something goes wrong with the circuit. Then our body seems to *short-circuit* and poor health develops.

Researchers have altered bioenergy fields through electrical and spiritual means. Scientists have done pioneering work in DNA manipulation using electrical frequency adjustments. Various authors are explaining medically and technically how energy effects can alter the intelligence and response of the human cell.

Today there is ever expanding interest in alternative methods of healing that range from religious practices to body manipulation techniques.

The Energy Of Thought

Most people have trouble letting go of their habits. When someone attacks our beliefs, in defense or retaliation, we fight back. This is human nature. However, words are potent weapons. Hence the "energy" effect of words needs to be understood.

Words are like *spears*. When you throw your words around you can do damage to someone, just like throwing a *spear* at them. You in turn can be wounded by the words of others. Starting in your childhood, you probably set up a defense mechanism against being wounded by other people's words or actions. I call this defense mechanism a *shield*.

You can construct *shields* through the power of your subconscious mind which adapts quickly to any endangering life situation to protect you. As you continue to *shield* yourself, you become very protected just like the armored knights of the Middle Ages. I call this sad condition the warrior mentality.

The warrior mentality becomes stronger and stronger

as you go through life and the armor-like *shields* become thicker. It becomes very difficult, to not be a warrior, because you instinctively fight back. One part of you wants to throw *spears* at your adversary (your words) while your subconscious mind erects *shields* to prevent others from hurting you!

As you continue to reinforce these protective *shields*, you slowly block out your own emotions. Sound familiar?

Servicemen will tell you that under combat conditions they can emotionally overload. To get through the war, carnage and loss of lives they blot out the emotional pain by building *shields*. Yet these same folks often suffer greatly after they return home because their body can not cope with remembering the war horrors. They often develop mental disorders, or are unable to function for a long time. This condition is called Post Traumatic Stress. Nightmares and flashbacks are common. (This condition can be effectively released without reliving trauma using the Process. And it can be done with multiple Recipient's simultaneously.)

Changing Our Behavior

In our original workshops we taught that changing our behavior is difficult. Every negative human encounter you have continues to thicken your *shields*.

Learning to lay down your *shields* is learning to let go.

To let go infers that it is possible to release yourself from whatever prevents you from being a whole, loving person—unafraid and not intimidated. A lasting change in behavior can only occur when you become aware of your attitudes and make a willful effort to operate differently in your daily life. For any change to occur, *you* must be willing to change or nothing can or will happen.

Efforts to dismantle *shields* can be successful using psychotherapy. However, it may take a long time and such help is not universally available to a population with many diverse needs. If you are receiving analysis or counseling, by all means continue to do so.

The Divine Love Group Healing Process will generally help you to clear your *shields* and change behavior easily and without pain.

Other Sources Of Illness

Where do you think illness comes from? There are many obvious means by which you can become ill. Through exposure to radiation, contaminants in air and water and food, drugs, plus genetic disorders and acquired diseases.

Other sources of illness can come from exposure to electronics. Studies have been done that suggest proximity to high voltage, microwaves and electro-magnetic fields can make people ill.

Surviving Chaos: Healing With Divine Love

Here is another source. Do you realize how powerful you are energetically? You have a definite impact on people. That impact can be positive or negative and can have good or bad effects upon you and the people around you.

When you think you create thoughts. Thoughts are energy bundles that can be transferred through space to someone else or stay in the immediate vicinity of your own body. I call stuck thoughts that are in or around us, *programs*. We will explore *programs* from the perspective of energy that affects your total being.

You can also be impacted by the directed thoughts of others! This occurs when you are in a hostile meeting. People can transfer their negative thoughts to you that can then stick to your bioenergy fields. Left intact, the thoughts seep into your system. The results are aches, tightness and muscle pains. Over a period of hours or weeks you may begin to feel poorly. We bet you have experienced these conditions. And now you know why! All of these issues are dealt with effectively with the DLGHP.

Blocking Spiritual Healing

The DLGHP is not blocked by a Recipient because the Petition used deals with mental resistance.

However, before I developed the Petition we had some people who continued to exhibit poor health despite their statements that they wanted to be well. If this has happened to you with a healer in the past, here are five conditions that may explain your continued poor health.

1. Your intellect - *You* can reject healing by the power of your own intellect. Anyone can do this by simply exercising their willpower. The rejection usually occurs on a conscious level when your education or experience causes you to doubt the reality of the healing. Sometimes rejection occurs when you struggle to set aside your disbelief and cannot because you are emotionally attached to your thoughts, such as a feeling of low self-worth.

2. Reinforced negative thoughts - People have been observed who failed to improve because they reinforced their own negative thoughts. They simply built a thought process that frustrated their health. For example, if you get more personal attention when you are unwell, you may choose unconsciously to stay ill.

3. Emotional triggers - Y*ou* can be triggered by emotional situations. Even a friend might trigger a *program* in you if there is an unresolved conflict within you. When you are subjected to an experience where old feelings are revived, your *mind*, working like a catcher's mitt, catches and holds the energy of thought directed to you by others. If those thoughts are hostile, your body can store that energy as a *program* and you can eventually find yourself with a health problem!

To break this cycle, you must be alert to your thoughts and feelings and take corrective action to release the unwanted *program* using the Process.

4. Expectations - As you grew up you were exposed to a variety of ideas about right and wrong. When you do not measure up to those standards, you may tend to punish yourself mentally. You may think that you are "unworthy" or that you are "inferior."

5. False logic - As you try to apply logic to your condition, you can find yourself on a circular path that locks you into your limited thinking. Any argument you make to yourself further convinces you that there is no solution to your problem. In effect you are on a mental merry-go-round with no way off.

Positive vs. Negative Thinking

Do you think it is important to maintain a positive outlook? It would be comforting to think that all your problems could be released through some kind of a healing process. I have found that such thinking is incorrect.

While it is true that you can release programs, you may also need to change your basic thinking. Otherwise over time you simply reinfect yourself with your own negative thinking or by the thinking of those around you. For example, if you think your coworkers are incompetent, you establish in your mind a negative thought that stays in your bioenergy field with your *catcher's mitt* waiting to catch additional negative thinking. The irony is these negative thoughts stay with you, gain strength and can interfere with your well-being.

We can name a negative behavior as a "symptom" and use the DLGHP to release that symptom and replace that departed energy with Divine Love. This usually rids a Recipient of continued negative thinking on a particular topic.

Stress And How To Deal With It

As we studied stress we learned two things:

First, stress can be transmitted between two people, even though one person was not originally in a stressful situation.

When you are in a meeting, the group's stress can be transferred to you without your conscious awareness. If you do not release the stress, your bioenergy fields can start to overload, and you can develop flu-like symptoms, be nauseous, or develop a headache.

Stress generated by others will not affect you if you really care about others. The Divine Love Group Healing Process will help you to be transparent to stress directed toward you.

Also, stress can be self-induced by your own thoughts and actions. This type of stress occurs when you deny your true-self or support a position contrary to your own belief system. Self-induced stress is minimal if your self-appreciation is intact. In other words, stress is retained in your body only when there is an "uncaring" program within *you* that concerns yourself or others.

If you observe your behavior carefully, you can learn to recognize and release the source of those stress causing incidents using the Process. Then you will find that previous situations that caused stress will have little effect upon you.

An Engineer's Interpretation Of Mind

At this point I want to explain an important principle to you about your mind. We have studied the release mechanism for many years that accompanies the departure of programs impeding health. As we evaluated results, we made a number of important observations that I want to share with you.

We have all heard that:

1. There are two parts to the mind, the active and the subconscious.

2. We use both parts of the mind simultaneously.

3. We are aware of our active thinking.

4. We are not aware of what our subconscious mind is doing.

Now let us explore how these four points apply as you go through life.

Your subconscious mind is like a moving picture camera constantly recording every experience you have from the moment of birth. Negative experiences are stored as well as the positive experiences.

The subconscious does another thing. It categorizes your negative experiences and then affects your current activities when a similar experience occurs. For example, if you have been mugged it would be very natural for you to develop an aversion to the national ity or race of your attacker. Quite often those negative experiences are so firmly embedded that you may view every future social encounter with suspicion.

You may purposely avoid dealing with people of a particular background or neighborhood because of the bad image your subconscious holds.

Any collection of bad experiences can trigger reactions in you to prevent decisions, impede success, frustrate fulfillment, or interfere with happiness in life. Each event compounds and adds to shields you construct for self-protection.

Two Examples - Past Client Problems Using Spiritual Love Without A Process Or Petition

1. A child did very well in school, but seldom saw his parents because they were always working. He grew up feeling unloved and grew up thinking that he was unlovable. He went to college and became a highly trained, unemotional machine. He was very successful in business at an early age, only to lose his business, home and marriage. He awoke one morning and realized that he felt nothing for anyone or anything. It took months to get him functioning again because he had to learn to accept the love of others.

2. A very successful doctor drove herself to excel and built a very large practice. She could not derive satisfaction from the service rendered to her patients. The doctor's *program* was that she had been repeatedly driven to despair as a child by parental comments that she was not good enough. She grew up thinking that she was not doing enough for her patients and drove herself to near collapse. After weeks of struggle she released *the not good enough program.* Then she started to experience the fulfillment that she sought from her profession.

Resistance to change - further need for a petition

Did you know that your mind has a built-in resistance to change? You are constantly being bombarded by change.

When you tend to overload because of stress, anxiety, or fast pace, your subconscious steps up its performance by protecting you from further damage. The subconscious does this by automatically blocking any energetic change from occurring. Then even if you want to drop a *shield* or *program*, the subconscious can block that action from taking place.

How often have you tried a self-improvement exercise – and after doing everything that was specified, you still did not get the desired results? The simple fact is your subconscious mind will resist any change threatening to your accumulated life history. This is also the reason why many self-healing techniques are temporary. You simply cannot break free.

By now you are probably wondering how to break the stranglehold of your subconscious mind. A doctor friend gave me a big clue many years ago, but I was not perceptive enough at the time to apply what he told me. He had many successes freeing people from eating and drinking disorders as part of a holistic regimen using vitamins, exercise, proper diet and an affirmation.

The affirmation was a simple sentence he told his

clients to repeat aloud ten times a day such as " I give up smoking." The doctor claimed that in thirty days his clients would no longer be addicted to cigarettes because the subconscious would reprogram itself to no longer want the cigarettes. When we first heard this claim, I really did not give it much credence.

A few years later one of my seminar participants was having a really tough time letting go of her *program* using an earlier version of this group healing process. *I suggested that she give herself verbal permission to change.* When she did so, her entire body started to shudder and she processed out of herself a limitation that had been holding her back in life.

Crazy you say? You bet, but that is how discoveries are made – by trying new ideas. From that point on I asked our clients to give themselves verbal permission to change and they did!

These events led me to the development and testing of the Petition and its wording.

More Lessons On The Word Called Love

You may think that love is something sexual, or a nonsexual feeling experienced only within your immediate family. If you have been brought up to not trust or care about your fellow man, it is very difficult to identify yourself with a concept you do not feel inwardly or understand.

To anyone who has been mentally or sexually abused, the word *love* just doesn't translate correctly because these people associate *love* with a beating or abuse.

When a child is beaten and then told that he or she is *loved* by a parent, confusion results. The child grows up associating abuse with love and generally selects a spouse that is an abuser or abused.

You cannot reach a person in this condition easily with words because he or she has already ingrained in their subconscious all of the wrong definitions of love.

Examples

Following are two examples where I was not using a process, but I was using my concept of personal Spiritual Love.

1. The Beaten Woman

A middle-age woman came to me for help. She was suffering from anemia and was not able to process minerals in her body. I tried to help her but nothing happened. I suspected a problem with her definition of personal spiritual love and asked her about her background. She had not been able to hold a steady job for fifteen years; she had been abused as a child; her ex-husband had beaten her regularly and he was

129

in jail for killing someone. I explained to her that the love we were using was our intention to help her unconditionally, without expecting anything in return except to experience that energy in a non-contact manner. I worked with her on several occasions and she eventually got better.

More important was the order of her recovery. First, she was able to see that all men were not evil and she was able to hold her first job in years. She started dating men and was happy with her relationships.

Second, all the physical conditions disappeared and she was able to maintain a proper mineral balance.

2. The Mentally Tortured Woman

Several years ago, a twenty-one year old woman was referred to me by her minister. The young woman was about to graduate from college with a degree in languages. She complained of a deep pain in her side.

I worked with her using my definition of personal spiritual love and got nowhere. Her minister later told me that this woman had been sent to the United States at age five to escape terrorism from her country's regime. As a child she did not understand the threat and got the idea that her parents no longer loved her because they had sent her away. She was told that upon graduation her visa was to be withdrawn and she was to return to he own country. She was terrified because many of her relatives had been assassinated and she feared for her own life. Do you understand the conflict she faced?

Her minister was able to explain to this woman that her parents had sent her to the United States because they did love her and wanted her to be safe. Once she understood that point she was able to adopt a definition of spiritual love that enabled me to help her.

In Conclusion

When I first started lecturing, I knew that there needed to be a pure intention for service, so I taught the use of *personal spiritual love*. Sometimes the results were limited or took a long time to realize.

After experiencing the long healing process that these two women had endured, I decided to surrender the entire healing ceremony to the Creator and started using Divine Love. Healing results improved and results were observed within minutes.

We hope that this background information helps you to understand and apply Divine Love in all that you do.

Feel free to write to us with your questions or comments. See the last page for our address.

"People who work together will win, whether it be against complex football defenses, or the problems of modern society."

Vince Lombardi

ABOUT THE AUTHOR

Bob Fritchie enjoyed a 40-year career as a professional chemical engineer and business manager.

In 1979 Bob formed a lifelong friendship with Marcel Vogel, a world renowned IBM scientist. Marcel, Bob and a team of dedicated professionals put together a research laboratory in San Jose, California. Once in place, the lab team began a scientific study of subtle energy healing principles. Bob also served on the Board of Directors and as business agent for the lab.

Marcel, Bob and others doctors affiliated with the lab taught these emerging energy principles through experiential workshops to help people heal their lives and health problems. The key teachings were based upon recognizing that the Creator's love is real and is an energy that can be experienced in our lives to clear us of many problems in the human condition.

Bob formed World Service Institute (WSI) as a nonprofit nondenominational teaching company to help the general public understand and apply Divine Love in resolving problems.

CONTACTING US

We can be reached by email at:

healinghelp@worldserviceinstitute.org

To inquire about a seminar in your area contact:

Meeting Coordinator
World Service Institute
P.O. Box 32801
Knoxville, TN 37930

Be sure to include your name, address, email and means by which you want to be contacted.

Visit the World Service Institute website at:

http://www.worldserviceinstitute.org

Ask your local bookstore to order your copies. Consult the 2009 edition of Books In Print for ordering details.